*Folger Documents of Tudor and Stuart Civilization*

# THE SCHOOLMASTER

# FOLGER DOCUMENTS

# OF TUDOR AND STUART CIVILIZATION

THIS volume is one of a series of publications of Tudor and Stuart documents that the Folger Library proposes to bring out. These documents will consist of hitherto unprinted manuscripts as well as reprints of rare books in the Folger Library. An effort will be made to choose significant items that will throw light on the social and intellectual background of the period from 1485 to 1715. In response to almost unanimous requests of interested historians, the spelling, punctuation, and capitalization will be modernized in printed texts. In some cases, where the original printing is clear and easily read, texts may be photographically reproduced. The Folger Library is prepared to supply microfilm of original texts to scholars who require a facsimile.

# THE
# SCHOOLMASTER
## (1570)
## BY ROGER ASCHAM

EDITED BY

*Lawrence V. Ryan*

PUBLISHED FOR

*The Folger Shakespeare Library*

BY

CORNELL UNIVERSITY PRESS

*Ithaca, New York*

*For my father and mother,*
*my first and best teachers*

# PREFACE

ALTHOUGH *The Schoolmaster* has been republished a number of times since the first post-Renaissance edition by James Upton (London, 1711), no modernization of the complete text is now in print. The present version is therefore intended to make accessible to contemporary readers, hopefully without changing too drastically its original Elizabethan character, a book that was one of the most influential Tudor educational treatises and at the same time an important landmark in the rise of modern English literary prose.

Among the many obligations incurred in preparing this volume, I should like to acknowledge my indebtedness to Professor Louis B. Wright, Director of the Folger Shakespeare Library, for encouraging the project; to Miss Virginia LaMar, also of the Folger Shakespeare Library, for her sensitive and meticulous editing of the manuscript; to Harvard University Press for permission to quote translations of a number of passages from authors in the Loeb Classical Library; to Stanford University Press for permission to use in the Introduction material from my earlier biography of Ascham (1963); and to the trustees of the Henry E. Huntington Library for permission to use their copies of the first edition of *The Schoolmaster* (1570) for pur-

*Preface*

poses of comparison in editing the text. I am deeply grateful to Mrs. Winifred Sleeper for the care with which she typed the manuscript. For his many kindnesses, I should like especially to thank Professor Kenneth B. Murdock, former Director of the Harvard University Center for Italian Renaissance Studies in Florence, because it was there, in the delightful surroundings of Villa I Tatti, that I completed most of the work on this edition of *The Schoolmaster*.

L. V. R.

*Stanford, California*
*December 2, 1965*

# CONTENTS

# INTRODUCTION

AMONG the many treatises on education produced by Englishmen during the Renaissance, two of the earliest to be written,
Sir Thomas Elyot's *The Governor* (1531) and Roger Ascham's
*The Schoolmaster* (1570), have enjoyed the widest and most
enduring fame. Throughout their own and much of the suc-
ceeding century the popularity of both authors was due largely
to their having set forth, in homely and robust prose, educational ideals and principles that appealed strongly to, as well as
did much to shape, the spirit of their time. For both Elyot and
Ascham were concerned with rearing an aristocracy capable of
assuming their proper social and political functions: namely, to
set the patterns of behavior for their countrymen, and to admin-
ister the kingdom wisely and justly under the Tudor monarchs.
Both writers, moreover, were sincere and learned humanists,
deeply committed students, that is to say, of those Greek and
Latin writers, Christian and pagan alike, in whose works the
Renaissance found inspiration for rejuvenating its own ethical,
political, and spiritual life.

For Ascham and Elyot, as for the Italian humanists and the
classical authorities who preceded and instructed them, the
chief natural means toward realizing the completely human life

was proper education. Nor was this task the exclusive concern of schools and universities. It was the business too, indeed the main business, of parents and, as Plato had declared, of every responsible member of society. As a consequence, both Ascham and Elyot wrote in their native tongue rather than in humanistic Latin in order to reach as wide an audience as possible. Hence their compatriots, not only their fellow scholars but also men and women competent in English alone, eagerly perused, imitated, and in many instances tried to put into actual practice the sound and clearly intelligible doctrine presented in *The Governor* and *The Schoolmaster.*

Although space is lacking here to record the substantial direct evidence of the esteem in which the two books were held and the influence they exerted on the writings of Ascham's and Elyot's compatriots, the facts of publication alone suggest their attraction for the reading public of Renaissance England. By 1580 *The Governor* had gone through eight editions, while within less than twenty years after its first appearance *The Schoolmaster* had gone through five.

Even though neither book contains highly original ideas on educational theory or method, in both the lay Elizabethan reader could discover for himself excellent doctrine on the bringing-up of youth that had been locked away from him hitherto in treatises composed in the learned languages. In Ascham's work especially he might discover, if he had never heard or had thought little of the matter before, the importance of such considerations as paying strict personal attention to the rearing of his children even from their infancy, since education begins in the cradle rather than in the schoolroom. He could discover, too, that praise is a better stimulus to learning than punishment; that systems of education are made for children and not children for the systems; that more is learned through apt illustration and cogent example than through rote memorization; that experience, particularly if raw and untutored, and

# Introduction

ill-supervised foreign travel are not invariably profitable and may even damage seriously the minds and characters of the young. No very startling revelations these, yet they stirred the hearts of Tudor readers, whose memories of their own ill rearing by overindulgent parents and harsh, unimaginative schoolmasters had often been unhappy. For however venerable and obvious some of them may seem, Ascham's ideas appealed and will continue to appeal to readers because many of them are, psychologically and pedagogically, of lasting value. They are presented, furthermore, in a prose that is pithy in phrasing and spiced with homely wit, with lively illustrative anecdotes concerning such fascinating contemporaries as the first Queen Elizabeth, the great Lord Burghley, and the unfortunate Lady Jane Grey. For these reasons, and because he expresses everything, the wrongheaded as well as the right and sound, with the full flavor of his own delightful individuality, the book which Ascham diffidently called his "poor schoolhouse" has found attentive and sympathetic readers in all generations since it first was published.

For the task of writing *The Schoolmaster* he was eminently qualified by both education and practical experience. The second son of John Ascham, a steward or overseer of estates to a prominent Yorkshire baron, Roger was born in the tiny village of Kirby Wiske, near Northallerton, in either 1515 or 1516. Here he apparently began his elementary education in the parish school, but at an early age he was placed in the household of Sir Humphrey Wingfield, a Suffolk jurist whose enlightened views on rearing children profoundly affected Ascham's own later educational theory and practice. For Sir Humphrey saw to it that the youths entrusted to his care were well founded in Latin and Greek by a kindly and able tutor, and he supervised their physical training himself. It was through his encouragement that the young Ascham developed a keen interest in archery that lasted throughout his life and gave him the matter for his

## Introduction

first published book, *Toxophilus* (1545), a eulogy of the English longbow and an argument for shooting with it as an ideal form of exercise and recreation for all men, but particularly for sedentary scholars in the university.

In 1530, Ascham went up to Cambridge, where he matriculated at St. John's College. Though a new foundation, the college was rapidly assuming, under the inspiration of scholars like John Redman and the youthful John Cheke, that leadership in Latin and, especially, Greek learning that had been concentrated in Oxford at the opening of the century. It was also becoming one of the liveliest centers of debate over the new theological writings of the German Protestants. Both the expanding knowledge of classical literature and the doctrines of the religious reformers attracted Ascham, who entered into his studies with such zeal that he soon made his mark as a youth to be reckoned with in the university. Besides pleasing his tutors with his accomplishments in languages, in mathematics, in music and drawing and fine penmanship, he moved ahead so rapidly as a scholar that he was able to try his hand, even before graduation, at instructing younger students in the fundamentals of Greek.

Upon receiving the baccalaureate degree in 1534, Ascham, though his outspoken expression of antipapal views jeopardized his chances with the religiously conservative majority within the society, was chosen fellow of St. John's. His good fortune, deserved because of his outstanding promise, had been insured by Nicholas Metcalfe, master of the college, who, as Ascham reports in *The Schoolmaster*, contrived in spite of his own staunch Catholicism to assure the election of the brilliant but brash young scholar. For fourteen more years Ascham remained at Cambridge without interruption except for illness and occasional journeys home. After receiving the master's degree in 1537, he lectured publicly in the schools of the university on the arts, including mathematics (for which he seems, incidentally, to have had no great respect) and his beloved Greek. Upon Cheke's appointment to the first regius professorship of Greek in 1540, Ascham became reader of the language in St. John's and, some years later, was rewarded for his accomplishments in the classical tongues with the public oratorship of the university.

During the golden earlier years of his career he achieved such notable success in instructing students within his college that his fame began to spread outside the academic world. Both Margaret Roper, daughter of St. Thomas More, and Lord Mountjoy, whose father had been a pupil of Erasmus and whose own household Ascham likened for patronage of learning to that of the Medici, tried to secure him as tutor for their children. But Ascham would have nothing to do with such offers, for Cambridge at the time seemed the most exciting and attractive place in England for an ambitious and zealous young scholar to be. There was a new zest for intellectual life in the university, exhibiting itself perhaps most prominently in the flourishing of Greek scholarship under the influence of Cheke and of Thomas Smith of Queen's College, Cheke's equal in ability if not in reputation as a student of the language and, like him, a leader in the academic struggle to have its pronunciation reformed. So much was Greek prospering that Ascham boasted in a letter to a fellow of St. John's who was absent at the time in Louvain, "Sophocles and Euripides are better known than Plautus was in former times when you were here. Herodotus, Thucydides, Xenophon are spoken of and borne in more hands than was Titus Livius then." It was also during these years that he formed a close companionship with Cheke and with the tragedian Thomas Watson, later Bishop of Lincoln, with whom he engaged in the literary conversations about the ancient historians and dramatists which he nostalgically recalls in *The Schoolmaster.*

Yet if his first decade at Cambridge was a happy one, during the 1540's his content and his scholarship were disturbed by a chronically recurring fever, religious faction at St. John's, and continuing disappointment of his hopes for high academic preferment. Some members of the university who were ill disposed toward him began dropping hints that he was a failure and a waster of precious time. These insinuations, of which he complains in his correspondence, along with his other personal difficulties led him to seek some means of convincingly proving his worth and at the same time to look out for patronage in some new manner of living. His treatise *Toxophilus,* in fact, seems to have been written to accomplish both these ends. With its stunning display of easily borne erudition and eloquent defense of physical recreation for the scholar, it is as much an apologia for his own career as it is a glorification of the strong yew bow of England.

Finally in 1548 came an offer attractive enough to draw him away from Cambridge. The Princess and future Queen Elizabeth had just lost her private tutor, William Grindal, a former pupil of Ascham's and his closest friend, who had died of the plague. The fifteen-year-old girl insisted upon having Ascham as a replacement, and he most willingly accepted the position. In entering her service at Chelsea Palace, he did not regard himself as having withdrawn from the university forever or as having undertaken an entirely new career. Nor was he completely unfamiliar with teaching in a royal household, for during the immediately preceding months he had been called at times to instruct the boy King Edward VI in the new Italic hand that he wrote with distinction himself. Directing Elizabeth's studies, moreover, was not really much different from tutoring boys in St. John's, where the typical undergraduate, as had been true of Ascham himself, was usually upon matriculation no older than the Princess. The greatest difference was probably, if the testimony of Ascham in *The Schoolmaster* and of others among his contemporaries does not exaggerate through flattery, that his new charge was far more intelligent and industrious than any pupil he had known in the university. This appointment marked the beginning for Ascham of studies with Elizabeth that were to continue, though with long intermissions, until his death over twenty years later. Upon his apt royal pupil he tried with great success some of his favorite pedagogical techniques, among them the process of "double translation" described in *The Schoolmaster,* the finest method ever devised, according to Ascham and other Renaissance authorities, for acquiring languages. He read with her from the best of the ancients, Greek in the mornings, Latin in the afternoons. Although he concentrated, because of the purity of their expression, upon the pagans Cicero and Livy, Sophocles, Isocrates, and Demosthenes, he did not neglect Christian writings in the classical tongues. The Princess' daily lessons began with a passage from the Greek New Testament, supplemented by such patristic authors as St. Cyprian. As a supporter of the Reformation, moreover, Ascham saw fit to add to her Latin exercises the *Loci communes rerum theologicarum* of the German theologian Philip Melanchthon.

From his account of her studies, it is clear that Ascham was trying to educate Elizabeth according to the best ideals of contemporary religious humanism. This means that he sought to develop her mind and character by combining the soundest and most fittingly expressed doctrine contained in the classics with the saving dogmas of religious faith. Having a nearly perfect subject to deal with, he hoped to fashion her into a learned and pious adult, suitably prepared to fulfill whatever role was destined to be hers in a Christian commonwealth. Thus, more than fifteen years before he began to compose his treatise, Ascham was trying out on the Princess the methods and attempting to realize in her the educational aims that were to form the main ingredients of *The Schoolmaster.*

Unfortunately, he had but a limited time and what proved to

be an unsuitable environment for carrying out his program. His pupil was under the guardianship of Henry VIII's widow, Catherine Parr, and her reckless and unprincipled husband Thomas Seymour, High Admiral of England and brother to the Lord Protector of the realm. Seymour, who had tried unsuccessfully to secure permission from the Privy Council to espouse the Princess after her father's death and then had suddenly contracted a secret marriage with Catherine, commenced to behave toward Elizabeth in a manner unbecomingly familiar for a guardian. Although for a while Catherine tolerated and even connived at her husband's unseemly behavior, eventually she protested, and within a few months after Ascham's arrival Elizabeth and her servants were packed off to live at Cheshunt, and later at Hatfield, in Hertfordshire.

Nor did the scandal end with this removal. In September, Catherine died in childbirth, and the scheming Seymour again considered marrying the Princess. This he meant to do clandestinely, for he was by now also plotting to discredit his elder brother with Edward VI and to replace him as Protector during the King's minority. When the Admiral was finally arrested in January, 1549, Elizabeth suffered the embarrassment of interrogation by an agent of the Privy Council and, though the investigator found nothing to implicate her in the intrigues for which Seymour was executed shortly afterward, she was kept in Hatfield in semiofficial disgrace by her brother for nearly two years.

Living in the midst of this scandal made Ascham well aware of how many temptations lay in wait for those who dwelt in royal households and how precarious was the courtier's career. When he writes in *The Schoolmaster*, therefore, of the dangers that beset susceptible youths at court and may unsuit them for honorable office, he is writing from intimate and painful experience and not merely quoting the usual commonplaces about the slipperiness of high place.

Not a word remains in his extensive correspondence, however, concerning the unfortunate circumstances of his life at Chelsea and Hatfield. The next that is heard from him is a letter to Cheke, dated from St. John's College, January 28, 1550, in which he reports his recent departure, or dismissal, from Elizabeth's household. Thus abruptly ended, in less than two years, his only period of official appointment as a royal tutor. A few years later, upon being recalled to court, he was to see that his teachings had by no means failed, but for the present he must have entertained some grave doubts about the success of his experiments.

Upon returning to Cambridge he reassumed his former university and collegiate duties, and he found some compensation for the loss of Elizabeth as a pupil in helping his friend Thomas Wilson with the tutoring of the young Duke of Suffolk and his brother, the sons of Henry VIII's favorite and onetime brother-in-law, Charles Brandon. He also became acquainted with the German Protestant theologian Martin Bucer. Through Bucer he formed an epistolary friendship, the most important of his life, with Johann Sturm, writer of influential educational treatises and rector of the much-admired *gymnasium* at Strasbourg. Although the two men were never to meet, they corresponded until Ascham's death eighteen years later, and Ascham rightly came to regard Sturm, along with his own teacher Cheke, as chief among contemporary begetters of the ideals expressed in *The Schoolmaster.*

This second period of Ascham's life in the university was destined to be very short. In September he was appointed secretary to Sir Richard Morison, the new English ambassador to the Emperor Charles V. After the visit to Lady Jane Grey described in the first book of *The Schoolmaster,* and another to Elizabeth in which the former pupil and tutor apparently became reconciled, he departed from London for Augsburg toward the end of the month. The account of his journey, preserved in letters to friends at home, is one of the earliest and most delightful bits of authentic English travel literature, for Ascham was an enthusiastic and perceptive tourist who seemed to miss nothing that was remarkable along his road into High Germany.

For the next three years, until the death of Edward VI, he was on the Continent, following the court and carefully observing the Emperor's fortunes through much of the disheartening final struggle with the French and with the German Protestant princes that preceded his abdication. Sojourning abroad provided the don from Cambridge with considerably broadened experience, a real taste, though a bittersweet one, of life among the mighty, and many new friends among the leading scholars of Germany and the Low Countries. It also supplied material for further epistolary accounts of his travels as well as for a number of revealing and historically significant observations upon famous personages of the day. Most important of all, it inspired him to undertake a history, unfortunately preserved only in a fragment, in which he tried to interpret current political developments in Germany according to the newest Continental methods of historiography. Finally, on the basis of a nine-days' visit to Venice, it gave him ammunition for the long diatribe against traveling to Italy that brings the first book of *The Schoolmaster* to a resounding conclusion.

In September, 1553, Ascham returned to England and, for a brief time, to Cambridge. The moment had now come to choose between a future in academia and at court, and with strong prompting from Bishop Stephen Gardiner, Lord Chancellor of England as well as Chancellor of the University, Ascham chose the court. Despite his undissimulated Protestantism, he became Latin Secretary to the Catholic Queen Mary. During this period he also married and so committed himself almost irrevocably to a public, rather than a university, career. At times during Mary's reign he was permitted to visit Elizabeth; upon these occasions he and his former pupil read Latin and Greek together, their favorite texts being the opposing orations of Demosthenes and Aeschines concerning the latter's notorious embassy for the Athenians to Philip of Macedon. Possibly they tried out on these orations Ascham's favorite exercise of double translation, but unfortunately their opportunities for meeting were too infrequent and brief for taking up once more a regular program of studies.

When Elizabeth succeeded her half sister on the throne in 1558, she too appointed Ascham her Latin Secretary. Since he held this post for the remainder of his life, he attended upon her almost daily and, whenever her official duties and his now-faltering health permitted, they continued their studies in Latin and Greek. Now, however, they were no longer master and pupil, and, as Ascham continued to read with her, he noted that the young Queen perfectly manifested, through her superior talent for languages and keen judgment of affairs, through her wise governance of England and model princely behavior, all that he had hoped she might become during his brief period as her girlhood tutor. Hence in *The Schoolmaster* he sets her forth as the pattern after which well-born youth ought to be fashioned, and it is noteworthy that his treatise owes its conception to a conversation he enjoyed with another courtier in her chamber at Windsor Castle, during a pause in their customary after-dinner reading of Demosthenes.

This conversation, according to Ascham's "Preface to the Reader," took place on an afternoon in December, 1563, when he and his interlocutor, Sir Richard Sackville, had just come from a lively debate over whether gentleness or severe discipline produces better results in educating the young. Upon Sackville's request to find him an ideal tutor for his grandson, Ascham hit upon the notion of writing a pamphlet on what to look for in both pupil and teacher, and in fact the course of their discussion, at least as he describes it from memory in his preface, is almost topic by topic an outline of the first half of

# Introduction

*The Schoolmaster.* This first part he had in draft within a couple of years, but then ill health and family concerns, among them serious complications in his financial affairs, kept him from bringing the work to completion. It is even possible that he never did finish the treatise, for the published version obviously lacks a considerable portion of the second book, and the only known manuscript is an earlier, slightly differing version of the first book only.[1] Ascham does claim in his final letter to Sturm, written during the latter part of 1568, that he had almost completed it except for certain details. Whether he did so or not before the year's end is not known, for on December 30 he died of a wasting fever, without having published or commented further on this, his most significant work. Nearly two years elapsed before it was set forth by his widow in its present form, incomplete either because part of the manuscript was lost in the interim or because Ascham had made no further progress on it after his report to Sturm.

Unfinished though it may be, there is still God's plenty in *The Schoolmaster.* While the title page suggests, correctly, that Ascham is concerned primarily with showing the way to fluency in Latin, the treatise, particularly in the first half, deals at large with fundamental principles of education. He had in fact written to Sturm of the two books that whereas the second was devoted to method, the first was mainly concerned with formation of character. Yet even the more technical latter half, though the running subtitle asserts its author's practical intent of "teaching the ready way to the Latin tongue," is remarkable not merely for expounding an excellent way of learning foreign languages, but also for a number of contributions it makes to literary theory and criticism.

[1] British Museum Royal MS. 18. B. xxiv, Article 2, completed before 1566, and perhaps before the end of 1564 (see George B. Parks, "The First Draft of Ascham's *Scholemaster,*" *Huntington Library Quarterly,* I [1938], 314–317).

# Introduction

In his views on pedagogy and the psychology of learning, and even to a considerable degree in his observations on literary craftsmanship, Ascham occupies an honorable and influential place in the evolving tradition of Renaissance educational theory and practice. This tradition, derived in its main features from the classics by such pioneering teachers of fifteenth-century Italy as Vittorino da Feltre and Battista Guarino, had been spreading thoughout Europe for more than a century, altering somewhat as it moved across the Alps in order to fit new and continually changing social, political, and religious conditions, yet maintaining over long distances and a long span of time the fundamental qualities that characterized it upon its first appearance in the princely courts of the Po Valley. The central aim of the humanist educators was to prepare youth for honorable service to society. And since most of them were concerned in the main with the offspring of the aristocracy, whose functions were to govern and to fight, they sought to mold the bodies, minds, and characters of their well-born charges so that they might be properly fit to exercise those offices that were their birthright. Their viewpoint was epitomized toward the very end of the period by the poet Milton: "I call therefore a compleate and generous Education that which fits a man to perform justly, skilfully, and magnanimously all the offices both private and publike of peace and war." [2]

Having in mind the destiny of most of their pupils to rule, or at least to advise rulers, the humanists fashioned their curriculum and system of moral discipline accordingly. Because of the ends that the humanists sought to achieve, and the fact that most of them wrote about the earlier rather than the more advanced stages of education, concern either with speculative knowledge for its own sake or with fitting the young for specialized professions is practically excluded from their letters and

[2] *Complete Prose Works*, gen. ed. Don M. Wolfe, II (New Haven, 1959), 377–379.

*Introduction*

treatises. Learning was becoming fashionable in Renaissance courts, but it was not the technical learning of the theologian, the physician, or the lawyer. Courtiers were becoming aware, rather, of a knowledge that could make them nobler in character and more cultured in manners and hence abler and more attractive as counselors to their princes. Princes in their turn were continually being reminded of the necessity for learning and excellent character in those who rule. "To be a philosopher and to be a Christian," wrote Erasmus in 1516 to the future Emperor Charles V, "is synonymous in fact. The only difference is in the nomenclature." [3]

No longer, therefore, did it suffice for the ideal nobleman to be a pious Christian, a valiant warrior, a pattern of good manners, and a possessor of certain social and artistic graces. All these he must still have, of course, but to them he must add the knowledge of affairs and the wisdom that can be acquired only by means of the right kind of learning. Hence the devout wish of Ascham in his treatise

that the youth in England, specially gentlemen, and namely nobility, should be by good bringing-up so grounded in judgment of learning, so founded in love of honesty as, when they should be called forth to the execution of great affairs in service of their prince and country, they might be able to use and to order all experiences, were they good, were they bad, and that according to the square, rule, and line of wisdom, learning, and virtue.

Further, as many of the educators thought, the aristocrat's religious life, since the society he was to serve as ruler or counselor was a Christian one, should manifest a learned rather than an unexamined and merely formal piety. *Pietas litterata* (an informed and articulate sense of devotion to one's duties) was the goal toward which both the kinds of studies and the

[3] *The Education of a Christian Prince*, trans. Lester K. Born (New York, 1936), p. 150.

system of moral discipline and edification advocated by most of the humanists were directed.

The liberal arts given most attention, consequently, were those that seemed likeliest to inculcate the ethical and political virtues. While there are variations in individual curricula, the subjects most commonly discussed and extolled in the writings of the humanists are grammar, rhetoric, poetry (that is, literature), history, and moral philosophy.[4] Grammar, by which is meant study of Latin and, often, also Greek, was indispensable, because the noblest thought of mankind, both pagan and Christian, was preserved in those two languages. Rhetoric, or the art of effective and persuasive speaking, came next, because it was believed that no one wanting in this talent could exert his proper influence in public affairs. History was studied for the actual, and poetry for the idealized or fictional, examples they presented of ethical and political conduct to be emulated or avoided. And finally came moral philosophy, because the wise man or woman must know the principles, as well as examples, of the good in order to choose unerringly the right path and hence exemplify the finest ideals of human character and behavior.

The inspiration for much of this educational program, though parts of it came down from the manuals of courtesy and "mirror for princes" literature of the Middle Ages, is classical, and the most influential authorities, as the reader can easily determine from Ascham's citations alone, include Plato's *Republic,* Aristotle's *Rhetoric, Nicomachean Ethics,* and *Politics,* Xenophon's *Education of Cyrus,* the pseudo-Plutarchan essay "On the Education of Children," Cicero's *De oratore,* and, above all the rest, the *Institutio oratoria* of Quintilian, which, after having been discovered in a complete version early in the fifteenth century, became the chief literary stimulus to many of the educational

[4] Paul Oskar Kristeller, *Renaissance Thought: The Classic, Scholastic, and Humanistic Strains* (New York, 1961), p. 10.

reforms of Renaissance humanism. For all of these ancient authors too were concerned with how to fit a man for a worthily active life in the state, whether as prince, senator, or citizen. Most of them, furthermore, looked not only for wisdom and goodness, but also for eloquence, in their ideally virtuous man. Nor were they ashamed in this enterprise to start at the beginning. Quintilian actually boasts of having devoted much of his attention, unlike others who professed to concern themselves with producing "the good man skilled in speaking"—the ideal Roman statesman—to the most formative, because most impressionable and tractable, earlier years of childhood.[5]

To the ideals that they found in their classical sources the Renaissance humanist educators nearly always added those of Christianity. Sometimes, it is true, their faith in the potentiality for goodness in human nature is so strong that their trust in the value of the "ethic and politic consideration" alone virtually eliminates the ingredient of revealed religion. But on the other hand, particularly in those countries of the North where the Reformation succeeded, the confidence in man's inborn disposition to the good is very often qualified by some firm reminder of his helplessness to perfect himself without divine assistance.

Thus Ascham on the one hand can rejoice that if "youth is fittest to all goodness, surely nature in mankind is most beneficial and effectual in this behalf," and on the other insist that even the best nature, without religion and grace, can never attain perfection in a truly human sense. Not even Cicero, Plato, and Aristotle, the authors among the ancients whom he, and most of his contemporaries, admired almost to idolatry, are in themselves sufficient. Taken along with sound Christian doctrine, they lead to uprightness and wisdom, but otherwise he regards even their writings as "but fine-edged tools in a fool's or madman's hand." This religious stress in Ascham's brand of humanism is further accompanied by an exceptionally noticea-

[5] *Institutio oratoria*, Proem 5.

# Introduction

ble flavor of nationalism, for while humanistic programs in general looked toward the prospering of the commonwealth, with Ascham the commonwealth is very specifically a Protestant England, so that in serving the state the properly fashioned gentleman was expected to serve the religion of England as well.

One sentence in the first book of *The Schoolmaster* quite neatly sums up Ascham's views and also explains the organization and peculiarities of emphasis of the treatise, particularly of the first book. "Therefore," he writes, after having marked out the signs of real capacity for learning in the young, "if to the goodness of nature be joined the wisdom of the teacher in leading young wits into a right and plain way of learning, surely children, kept up in God's fear and governed by his grace, may most easily be brought well to serve God and country both by virtue and wisdom." This "right and plain way of learning," as the opening paragraphs of the book make clear, is in the narrower sense a royal road to competence in Latin, key to the first of the two richest treasuries of learning. Here Ascham is quite unlike his predecessor Elyot, who considers at length and in great detail the whole curriculum and system of moral discipline, especially the five liberal studies that typify the humanistic program. Yet Ascham, though he is writing rather from the standpoint of an experienced and successful tutor in languages than from that of the educational psychologist or philosopher, is clearly aware that his method, excellent as it may be in itself, is not enough. Almost immediately the argument shifts from a question of technique into what is meant by intellectual aptitude in the child and what constitutes wisdom for the master in dealing with the pupils entrusted to his care.

The concern of almost half of Book I is consequently to mark out the characteristics of an apt child and to suggest what are the best means of alluring such a favored person to diligence in his studies. Ascham regrets that almost no parents and few masters know how to recognize true capacity when they see it. Hence the long comparison of "quick and hard wits," of the false prodigy who is too often praised and the less flashy but far sounder type of boy whose unwillingness to bend as the wind blows is too often mistaken by the undiscerning as intractability or dullness. Ascham acknowledges that real geniuses, such as was his old friend Cheke, may be also quick and pliable, but it distresses him that the superficially brilliant frequently carry away all the honors, while others who are really more capable and deserving are not encouraged by any praise to further efforts. Contrariwise, it happens too that gentlefolk, who ought to be its chief supports because it is their mission to help the prince govern the kingdom wisely, undervalue learning. They mistakenly keep their abler sons away from books and pack the least capable off to the university as "good enough to become a scholar." At this point Ascham first definitely exhibits his patriotic concern: how are learning and hence England and religion to be well served if no better care is taken to find out truly good natures for study?

To help in this task of detecting real promise, he marks out seven Platonic "true notes" of a "good wit." Then, having labeled and described them, he warns parents and schoolmasters that such gifts of nature may be spoiled by mishandling. With this monition begins the famous passage on gentleness in education, which culminates in the charming anecdote about Ascham's last conversation with Lady Jane Grey. He deplores, as did his great model Quintilian long before him, and as James Joyce has done so movingly in the present century, the brutal but apparently immortal practice of trying to pound learning into children. Ascham proposes that "gentle allurements" be tried instead. What is made pleasurable to a child will attract him; he can only be repelled by pain. The young do not by nature prefer sports to study; if the classroom were made "a

*Introduction*

sanctuary against fear," as Lady Jane Grey's tutor had made it for her, they would set themselves to learning enthusiastically.

Until Book II, Ascham says little about what he would have children study. Instead he turns next to the matter of their moral training. That he devotes so much more space in the first book to character than he does to intellectual matters simply reflects a tendency of many Renaissance writers on education, for whom moral excellence in both pupil and master was the *sine qua non*. Even the latter was to be selected chiefly for his goodness and then, as Elyot had asserted, "if he be also learned, he is the more commendable." [6]

If gentlefolk are feckless about the intellectual training of their children, Ascham insists that they are even worse botchers of their moral upbringing. Parents are too indulgent, often, as his account of the four-year-old past master in profanity is meant to show, bending their offspring toward vice rather than virtue by ill example and by conniving at their vanities. He regrets that English youth are allowed too much rein, especially in the dangerous years of early manhood. Unlike such writers as Montaigne, he would not have a young gentleman "boldly be made fit for all nations and companies, even for dissoluteness and excess, if need be." [7] For Ascham, experience is too painful and wasteful a teacher. "Learning," he claims, "teacheth more in one year than experience in twenty, and learning teacheth safely, when experience maketh more miserable than wise."

Such an assertion does not mean that he wants to make a dull bookworm out of his young gentleman. He insists, being himself an affable man with a love of pastime and good company, upon the need of all for pleasant and honest recreation. In preparation for his active future life, the youth should participate in "all pastimes generally which be joined with labor, used in open

[6] *The Governour*, ed. H. H. S. Croft (London, 1883), I, 36.
[7] Michel de Montaigne, "Of the Education of Children," *The Complete Works*, trans. Donald M. Frame (Stanford, 1957), p. 123.

place and on the daylight, containing either some fit exercise for war or some pleasant pastime for peace," all such, that is, as "be not only comely and decent but also very necessary for a courtly gentleman to use." It is neglect not only of learning but also of exercises becoming to their station in life that has caused the good influence of the nobility to decline. Because so many among them "have been either drowned in vain pleasure or overwhelmed by stout willfulness," the rest of society too has become disordered. He hopes, therefore, that those who are born to govern will not ape the vainest fashions of the court but will follow instead the example set by their illustrious queen in preparing herself to rule. Then they might perceive that " 'how great soever they be now by blood and other men's means, they shall become a great deal greater hereafter by learning, virtue, and their own deserts, which is true praise, right worthiness, and very nobility indeed.' "

Ascham's discussion of moral upbringing is capped by the long diatribe against Italy. He would spare all young men the danger to their character and religion of Italian books and travel. Though he had once longed to visit Italy more than any other country, he can now find nothing to commend about it except the beauty of its language. Undoubtedly his animus was due to such things as the association of Italy with papistry, the recent spate of translations of "bawdy" Italian *novelle*, and the Italianate manners brought back to England by some of his more impressionable countrymen. This notion of Italy as a place of Circean enchantment was hardly new with Ascham, but his is the most vigorous and memorable expression of a prejudice that was shared by many Elizabethans and is by no means dead among English-speaking peoples even today.[8]

If little of this material is particularly original, much of it

[8] For some examples of Tudor mistrust of travel into Italy, see the notes to John E. B. Mayor's edition of *The Scholemaster* (London, 1863), pp. 222–223.

nevertheless has perennial and not merely historical interest to readers seriously concerned with the proper ends and means of education. Ascham, besides, presents his case, even where he expresses quite obvious or dubiously valid opinions, through such arresting language that one is usually willing to lend him an attentive ear. It matters little to the reader who comes upon them with a delightful sense of discovery that some of the best passages, including those on "quick and hard wits" and on the irony of valuing horse trainers more highly than schoolmasters, were already commonplaces in Ascham's day. Indeed it mattered very little to Ascham and his contemporaries, for whom the important thing in a writer was not complete originality in ideas, but rather fresh and persuasive assertion of fundamental and reassuring truths.

One need only turn to the second half of *The Schoolmaster* for explicit evidence of this attitude. Having established his views on intellectual and moral discipline in general, Ascham returns to the avowed main purpose of "this book of the first principles of grammar." If his doing so seems a constriction, the reader must bear several facts in mind while proceeding through the remainder of the treatise. Ascham is writing, first of all, about the private education of children, prior to their going up to the university. Before they can engage in more advanced studies they obviously need to become competent in Latin and acquire, where possible, some foundation in Greek. Ascham's own forte, from his youth at Cambridge onward, had been skill in teaching both languages, and it is not only characteristic of him as an author but also natural, in view of Sackville's request, that he should write about these things that he knew best. Furthermore, grammar in his day was a term conceived in a much broader sense than it is in our own time. The *grammarius* was, for all practical purposes, equivalent to a professor of humanities, assigned the responsibility not merely of teaching the rudiments of language, but also of introducing his charges

# Introduction

to the writings of the ancient poets, dramatists, orators, historians, and often the moral philosophers. Evidence of this function is the considerable space devoted by Ascham to criticism, in ethical as well as linguistic terms, of a number of major classical authors in these various genres.

It is true, finally, that in the slogan *pietas litterata* both Ascham and Sturm, from whom he inherited the ideal, looked upon the attributive *litterata* as no less important than the substantive *pietas*. In this respect they resemble their models Quintilian and Cicero, who in effect stressed excellence in discourse (*bene dicere*) more vigorously than they did right conduct (*bene vivere*). The idea underlying such an emphasis is that in human affairs virtue exerts little influence when unaccompanied by force of eloquence; Sturm and Ascham, besides, sincerely believed that where small attention is paid to manner of expression, sound learning and morality are often displaced by error and frivolity.[9] As a consequence, they have sometimes been dismissed as less broadly humane in their interests than other leading Renaissance educational theorists, and the second part of *The Schoolmaster* has frequently been ignored or read inattentively even by admirers of the first. Yet if Ascham seems in it to have narrowed his field of vision and to be stressing unduly the importance of acquiring a Latin style patterned after that of Cicero, this part of his work was highly regarded well into the eighteenth century, and it remains valuable for the insight it affords into the practical teaching methods employed by some of the more enlightened educators of the age. No less significant is what it reveals about some typical approaches to

[9] See below, pp. 84, 115–116, and Sturm: "But knowledge of things without grace in discourse is wont to be barbarous and vile, and likewise with the corruption of speech we observe that a kind of captious conviction of their own wisdom steals unto men. Whence it may be seen that the first tender age of children ought to be given over to instruction in proper speaking" (editor's translation from *De literarum ludis recte aperiendis liber* [Strasbourg, 1543], sig. 4v).

literature and to problems of literary composition in a time when the writer looked upon his craft from a point of view not entirely like our own.

Of the half-dozen ways cited by Ascham for mastering Latin, he holds with but two—*translatio linguarum* (double translation) for beginning pupils and *imitatio* (shaping one's own style upon the finest models) for the more proficient. He insists that double translation, into English from a worth-while Latin text, preferably selected from Cicero, and, after a respite, back into Latin again, is the only swift and sure method for the younger scholar. As proof that it excels rote grammatical study and all the other ways recommended by the "best heads"—*paraphrasis, metaphrasis, epitome,* and *declamatio*—he cites what it had done for Queen Elizabeth and also the amazing progress made with it by a young gentleman whom he had known while serving as her tutor.[10]

Because he objects to them for various reasons, Ascham would have his schoolmaster rule out three of the remaining methods, and, since his work is unfinished, he says nothing whatsoever about the other, *declamatio.* By far the major part of Book II is therefore devoted to *imitatio,* the ideal, or rather the only exercise, in his opinion, for bringing one's Latinity to perfection. This grammatical imitation, as distinguished from dramatic μίμησις, he defines as "a faculty to express lively and perfectly that example which ye go about to follow." Here he does not have in mind merely slavish aping of the mannerisms of one's original. Taking their cue from the reasonable judgment of Quintilian on the matter, none of the more intelligent advocates of imitation regarded the process in such a light. For

---

[10] For a helpful outline of the method of double translation see the introduction to Edward Arber's edition of *The Scholemaster* (Birmingham, 1870), pp. 9–11. T. W. Baldwin also discusses the method in considerable detail in *William Shakspere's Small Latine & Lesse Greeke* (Urbana, 1944), I, 261–275.

## Introduction

Ascham's master on the subject, Sturm, imitation is rather "a forceful and artistic inclination of mind" to rival, not merely to follow, one's model, and to transmute everything drawn upon into an achievement that is distinctly one's own.[11] In advocating the process as a means to perfecting one's own learning and style, Ascham thus simply reflects what was felt to be obvious in his own time and for nearly two centuries thereafter: man is a creature whose information comes first through his senses and who learns by imitating what he observes in the world around him. "All the works of nature," Ascham declares, "in a manner be examples for art to follow." The same may be said of the works of man, products of art working upon the stuff of nature; the only conceivable point of dispute is not over whether one should imitate, but simply over which example or examples are the best to follow.

Ascham makes it unmistakably clear that for studying Latin prose there is only one answer, Cicero. In doing so he places himself, though neither his own Latin nor his English style is excessively Ciceronian, among the stricter disciples of the leading Roman orator. Almost no Latinist in the Renaissance would have doubted the worth of Cicero as a model; authors and rhetoricians of the age split into opposing parties and fought bitterly for decades solely over the issue of whether he alone was to be imitated or not. For this reason Ascham explains in detail why no other Latin prose writer of "the best age"—Varro, Sallust, or even the nearly perfect Caesar—will serve as an ideal pattern. Unfortunately the text breaks off in the middle of his discussion of Caesar, so that we do not know how he would have justified his exclusive choice of Cicero. Equally unfortunate is his failure to explain sufficiently how one ought to go about the business of imitation. He does mention his eagerness

---

[11] *Ioannis Sturmii de imitatione oratoria libri tres* (Strasbourg, 1574), sigs. A4r, B2v.

to see completed Sturm's hopefully definitive treatment of the subject, and he promises, since no one else appears willing to perform the task, to collect a volume of excellent specimens of imitation himself.

Yet even though death prevented his fulfilling the promise, there is enough in Book II of *The Schoolmaster* about imitation to give some clue to its lasting influence on the teaching of Latin in English schools. Throughout most of the two following centuries imitation is recommended as the chief means of improving one's Latin, and even one's vernacular, style; such influential writers of educational treatises as Henry Peacham and John Locke, for example, were convinced that the best way to eloquence in English was through following the choicest classical authors.

One of the most revealing bits of evidence concerning the great importance attached to the process and Ascham's major role in giving it broad currency comes from one of its dispraisers. Sir Francis Bacon, in reflecting upon his own distasteful experience of Elizabethan Cambridge, blamed Sturm and Ascham in particular for the "infinite and curious pains" that were being still expended upon Ciceronian imitation, which he disparages as a "delicate and polished kind of learning." [12] For Ascham, though not the first to urge the practice upon his countrymen, proved to be the author to whom they paid most heed and the one who most frequently came into their minds whenever they praised and advocated imitation of the ancients as the surest way to eloquence. Perhaps two of the finest tributes to his influence, on both Latin and English style, came from the eighteenth, rather than his own, century. William Elstob, editor of Ascham's Latin epistles (London, 1703), writes in his dedication that he is making them available once more to show schoolboys what proper imitation of Cicero can

---

[12] Preface to "The Advancement of Learning," *Works*, ed. James Spedding *et al.*, new edition, III (London, 1887), 284.

do for one's Latinity.[13] And later in the century Samuel Johnson told a friend that he had developed his own prose style "through study of Ascham and others." [14]

Even if the latter part of *The Schoolmaster* had accomplished no more than thus to show why the classics were especially prized and how they were interpreted and exploited by Renaissance teachers of youth, it would be valuable for the intellectual historian. Though Ascham protests that he busies himself about *imitatio* only as a means "for learning of tongues and sciences," his work becomes more than a grammarian's vade mecum; in an important sense it becomes also a critical treatise and a manual of literary craftsmanship.

Granted that the literary criticism to be found on these pages is only incidental to the main argument, it is sufficient in scope and interest to justify calling *The Schoolmaster* the first influential document of English neoclassicism. The stress on following Greek and Roman models in composition, treating matter like theirs in a dissimilar manner, or subjects unlike in a similar way, shades over quickly from grammatical and rhetorical to literary theory and practice. Thus Ascham chooses as his prime instance of imitation how "Virgil followed Homer, but the argument to the one was Ulysses, to the other Aeneas." It seems significant that he places this example from poetry immediately before, rather than after, that of Cicero's attacking "Antony with the same weapons of eloquence that Demosthenes used before against Philip." Not only the insistence upon imitation, but the very indifference to distinguishing sharply between rhetoric and poetics, along with the keen concern over formal and linguistic matters, typifies much of the literary theorizing and

[13] Quoted in *The Whole Works of Roger Ascham,* ed. J. A. Giles, I (London, 1865), cx.

[14] *The Critical Opinions of Samuel Johnson,* ed. Joseph Epes Brown (Princeton, 1926), pp. 281–282.

actual practice of Ascham's own and the immediately following ages.

Besides outlining and demonstrating the use of a method for analyzing examples of imitation, a method that still remains an essential tool of the critic, Ascham also expresses opinions on the literary strengths and weaknesses of a number of classical authors, on the ancient versus contemporary drama, and on the making of verse. His estimate of certain writers and the reasons for which he valued or dispraised them, precisely because he was both echoing the opinions of earlier contemporaries and helping to shape those of the coming generation, tell the reader much about how the classics were read and discussed during the sixteenth century. As might be expected, he praises the giants—Plato, Aristotle, Homer, Virgil, Demosthenes, and Cicero—without qualification, but his judgments about other authors are more interesting. His admiration for the historians— Herodotus, Thucydides, Livy, Sallust, Polybius, and Caesar—in a sense merely reflects the humanistic enthusiasm for history as a branch of knowledge indispensable to the cultivated man. In keeping with the main purpose of his treatise, however, his comments on these historians as writers of prose tell much about how they were regarded in his time and why some were studied more intensively than others. For instance, the prose of Sallust and of Thucydides, to whom he prefers Herodotus, he finds regrettably bookish and "outlandish," whereas for "propriety in words, simplicity in sentences, plainness, and light," Caesar and Livy "are perfect examples of imitation." The Elizabethan schoolboy may have studied Greek and Roman histories because they held a mirror up to man in his political nature, but the texts to which he was exposed were chosen largely for the quality of the style in which were depicted the examples of conduct that he was expected to emulate or avoid.

Ascham treats the poets from much the same point of view. From them may be learned pure Latin speech, even from

*Introduction*

Catullus, whom, despite his unsuitable matter, Ascham commends for "deserving well of the Latin tongue." The same is true for Plautus and Terence, whose themes he considers "base stuff for that scholar that should become hereafter either a good minister in religion or a civil gentleman in service of his prince and country." Yet if carefully selected, both, especially Terence, are excellent for the language. Although one might too readily conjecture in our day that such an approach to the Roman and Greek classics would kill off the pupil's interest, it seems rather that this close attention, even in excerpts and snippets, to the style of the ancient historians and poets gave Tudor schoolboys a real sense of how language works in literature as well as the means to profit in their own adult writing from the inspiration of the classics.

The rest of what Ascham has to say about the drama is more strictly literary criticism in the usual sense of the term than are his comments on Plautus and Terence. When he comes to tragedy, he prefers the Athenians to Seneca and so manifests, not merely a snobbishness about things Greek, but a desire to turn English playwrights from an inferior model to better ones. In his discussion of the drama, moreover, he shows himself to be the first English author who is acquainted with the *Poetics* of Aristotle. He takes "Aristotle's precepts" as his own criteria for dramatic excellence, and he even supports, against the usual current of the time, Aristotle's views that Euripides is a more moving writer than Sophocles and that tragedy is a higher form of poetry than the epic. Although most Elizabethan popular playwrights were to pay little heed to what either Ascham or Aristotle said, preferring to go on writing as romantically and melodramatically as they and their audiences chose, *The Schoolmaster* does contain the first authentic English criticism of the stage. It is criticism, moreover, that was to enter, through its influence upon Sir Philip Sidney, into the lively controversies

## Introduction

of the next generation over the deficiencies of the contemporary theater.

Perhaps the most curious passage in Book II for the modern reader is the discussion concerning whether or not the vernacular poet should employ rhyme. In advocating a verse measured by classical principles of syllabic quantity rather than stress and insisting that serious authors eschew "rude, beggarly rhyming," Ascham may seem to be merely a crank or a zealot in a hopeless cause. The whole Elizabethan controversy over the issue of rhyme has sometimes been dismissed by historians of literature as a purely academic sideshow having little to do with actual literary performance. Yet while one must grant that Ascham and other advocates of quantitative measures often achieved little more than "passing pitiful hexameters" themselves and committed even greater barbarities in the name of superior classical taste, the discussion and experiment did have certain important and salutary consequences for English verse. To Ascham, though he did not live to see its outcome, must go much of the credit for stirring up the debate, and the influence of his prejudices can be found in so late a passage as Milton's defense of the use of blank verse in *Paradise Lost*. The notion, too, of a possible constant for verse other than rhyme, or rather of one in addition to the then very imperfectly understood principle of stress, is not to be judged by the frightful example of some of Ascham's own poor efforts. Far better poets than he, among them Sidney and Spenser, did take up his hints and learned through their own experiments how to achieve splendid variation of movement in verse by counterpointing accent against quantity. With good sense and taste, moreover, they effectively ended the debate by perfecting native equivalents for the classical measures, such as the decasyllable for heroic and tragic poetry, or Ben Jonson's exquisite tetrameter couplets, matching in grace and flexibility, though not directly copying,

## Introduction

the meters of the ancient lyrics and epigrams that inspired much of his finest verse.

*The Schoolmaster,* though by no means a masterpiece of either humanistic thought or artistic prose, is nevertheless a rich storehouse of both admirable and strange Elizabethan ideals. Its achievements and its limitations alike typify much of the educational and literary theory and practice of the Tudor and Stuart ages. And apart from its undeniable historical interest, Ascham's treatise will continue to attract thoughtful readers through its generally "plain and sensible utterance" on educating the young.

## Note on the Text

*The Schoolmaster* was first published by John Day at London in 1570. New editions by Day appeared in 1571, 1573, and 1579; a fifth was brought out by Abel Jeffes in 1589. The first post-Renaissance edition was that of James Upton (London, 1711; "revised and enlarged," London, 1743). Since then, the treatise has been reprinted a number of times, both separately and in the collections of Ascham's works by James Bennet (London, 1761), J. G. Cochrane (London, 1815), Dr. J. A. Giles (London, 1864–1865), and William Aldis Wright (Cambridge, 1904). The standard edition is John E. B. Mayor's (London, 1863; reprinted 1884, 1892). The treatise has also appeared in Arber's English Reprints (London, 1870; Westminster, 1895), in Cassell's National Library (London, 1900; New York, 1902), and, most recently, in an edition by D. C. Whimster (London, [1934]).

The present modernization is based on a copy of the first edition owned by the Folger Shakespeare Library. This edition, publication of which was supervised by Ascham's widow, may be considered the most authoritative. No major bibliographical

*Introduction*

difficulties are introduced in subsequent early printings of the treatise, though in a few instances I have used the 1571 edition to correct minor errors occurring in the version of 1570.

In preparing the text, I have modernized the spelling and punctuation and have suppressed capital letters and italics where present convention would not demand them. I have also broken up a few of Ascham's longer periods and incorporated some of his shorter elliptical sentences into others in order to conform with modern usage. Ascham's characteristically heavy pointing has presented some difficulty, for, despite its variation from modern practice, he often used it effectively to call attention to rhythmical and logical relationships in his highly patterned sentences. I have decided, nevertheless, to lighten the punctuation on the grounds that the original system would appear quaint in an otherwise modernized version. Readers who are curious about its relationship to his prose style may consult the 1570 text or Wright's edition of Ascham's *English Works*.

Although Ascham often quotes his authorities from memory or from imperfectly edited texts, I have not altered his quotations except to correct obvious misspellings or, in passages of Greek, misplacing of accents. Further, I have supplied translations in the notes only where the original Latin or Greek is neither translated nor paraphrased by Ascham himself. Wherever possible, the translation has been taken from the version in the Loeb Classical Library; citations of classical passages have also been given, for the greater convenience of the reader, according to the systems adopted by the editors of the Loeb texts.

In order not to overburden this edition with critical apparatus, I have identified persons mentioned by Ascham only where additional facts may be necessary to place the reference meaningfully in context or to prevent confusion for the reader. Further information about all significant personages alluded to by Ascham may be found in standard encyclopedic or bibliographical reference works. To avoid peppering the text with distracting punctuation marks, I have expanded without brackets or other indication such titles as *M.* for *Marcus* or *Master* and *D.* for *Divus* or *Doctor,* and I have likewise substituted the modern equivalents for obsolete spellings. Not always have I altered, however, archaic or dialectal forms of certain words. In all cases of emendation where there is the slightest doubt about Ascham's meaning, I have supplied the 1570 reading in the notes. Except where erroneous attribution has required editorial comment, I have ignored the marginal notes in the original edition, since many of them are mere indicators or "pointers" of the type that often abound in Renaissance manuscript and printed works.

# THE
# SCHOOLMASTER

Or plain and perfect way of teaching children,
to understand, write, and speak the Latin tongue,
but specially purposed for the private bringing-up
of youth in gentlemen's and noblemen's houses,
and commodious also for all such as have forgot
the Latin tongue, and would, by themselves,
without a schoolmaster, in short time,
and with small pains, recover a
sufficient ability to understand,
write, and speak Latin.

## By Roger Ascham.

## An. 1570

At London.
Printed by John Day, dwelling
over Aldersgate.

*Cum Gratia & Privilegio Regiae Majestatis,
per Decennium.*

To the honorable Sir William Cecil, Knight, Principal
Secretary to the Queen's Most Excellent Majesty

Sundry and reasonable be the causes why learned men have
used to offer and dedicate such works as they put abroad to
some such personage as they think fittest, either in respect of
ability of defense, or skill for judgment, or private regard of
kindness and duty. Every one of those considerations, sir, move
me of right to offer this my late husband's Master Ascham's
work unto you. For well remembering how much all good
learning oweth unto you for defense thereof, as the University
of Cambridge, of which my said late husband was a member,
have in choosing you their worthy Chancellor acknowledged;
and how happily you have spent your time in such studies and
carried the use thereof to the right end, to the good service of
the Queen's Majesty and your country to all our benefits;
thirdly, how much my said husband was many ways bound
unto you, and how gladly and comfortably he used in his life to
recognize and report your goodness toward him, leaving with
me, then, his poor widow, and a great sort of orphans a good
comfort in the hope of your good continuance, which I have
truly found to me and mine, and therefore do duly and daily
pray for you and yours—I could not find any man for whose
name this book was more agreeable for hope [of] protection,
more meet for submission to judgment, nor more due for respect of worthiness of your part and thankfulness of my husband's and mine. Good, I trust, it shall do, as I am put in great
hope by many very well learned that can well judge thereof.

3

## The Schoolmaster

Meet therefore I count it that such good as my husband was able to do and leave to the commonweal, it should be received under your name, and that the world should owe thank thereof to you, to whom my husband the author of it was, for good received of you, most dutifully bounden. And so, beseeching you to take on you the defense of this book, to advance the good that may come of it by your allowance and furtherance to public use and benefit, and to accept the thankful recognition of me and my poor children; trusting of the continuance of your good memory of Master Ascham and his; and daily commending the prosperous estate of you and yours to God, whom you serve and whose you are, I rest to trouble you.

Your humble MARGARET ASCHAM.

# *A Preface to the Reader*

WHEN the great plague was at London, the year 1563, the Queen's Majesty Queen Elizabeth lay at her castle of Windsor, where, upon the tenth day of December, it fortuned that in Sir William Cecil's chamber, Her Highness' principal secretary, there dined together these personages: Master Secretary himself, Sir William Petre, Sir John Mason, Doctor Wotton, Sir Richard Sackville, Treasurer of the Exchequer, Sir Walter Mildmay, Chancellor of the Exchequer, Master Haddon, Master of Requests, Master John Astley, Master of the Jewel House, Master Bernard Hampton,[1] Master Nicasius,[2] and I. Of which number the most part were of Her Majesty's most honorable Privy Council and the rest serving her in very good place. I was glad then, and do rejoice yet to remember, that my chance was so happy to be there that day in the company of so many wise and good men together as hardly then could have been picked out again out of all England beside.

Master Secretary hath this accustomed manner, though his head be never so full of most weighty affairs of the realm, yet at dinnertime he doth seem to lay them always aside and findeth

[1] Clerk of the Privy Council.
[2] Nicasius Yetswaert, an agent for Queen Elizabeth in the Netherlands.

ever fit occasion to talk pleasantly of other matters, but most gladly of some matter of learning, wherein he will courteously hear the mind of the meanest at his table.

Not long after our sitting down, "I have strange news brought me," saith Master Secretary, "this morning, that divers scholars of Eton be run away from the school for fear of beating." Whereupon Master Secretary took occasion to wish that some more discretion were in many schoolmasters in using correction than commonly there is. Who many times punish rather the weakness of nature than the fault of the scholar. Whereby many scholars that might else prove well be driven to hate learning before they know what learning meaneth, and so are made willing to forsake their book and be glad to be put to any other kind of living.

Master Petre, as one somewhat severe of nature, said plainly that the rod only was the sword that must keep the school in obedience and the scholar in good order. Master Wotton, a man mild of nature, with soft voice and few words, inclined to Master Secretary's judgment and said, "In mine opinion, the schoolhouse should be indeed, as it is called by name, the house of play and pleasure,[3] and not of fear and bondage. And as I do remember, so saith Socrates in one place of Plato.[4] And therefore if a rod carry the fear of a sword, it is no marvel if those that be fearful of nature choose rather to forsake the play than to stand always within the fear of a sword in a fond[5] man's handling." Master Mason, after his manner, was very merry with both parties, pleasantly playing both with the shrewd touches of many curst boys and with the small discretion of many lewd[6] schoolmasters. Master Haddon was fully of Master Petre's opinion and said that the best schoolmaster of our time

[3] *Ludus literarum* (marginal note).

[4] Plato, *Republic*, VII.537A: "Do not, then, my friend, keep children to their studies by compulsion but by play."

[5] Foolish.      [6] Ignorant.

6

## A Preface to the Reader

was the greatest beater, and named the person.[7] "Though," quoth I, "it was his good fortune to send from his school unto the university one of the best scholars indeed of all our time, yet wise men do think that that came so to pass rather by the great towardness of the scholar than by the great beating of the master. And whether this be true or no, you yourself are best witness." I said somewhat farther in the matter, how and why young children were sooner allured by love than driven by beating to attain good learning—wherein I was the bolder to say my mind because Master Secretary courteously provoked me thereunto, or else, in such a company, and namely in his presence, my wont is to be more willing to use mine ears than to occupy my tongue.

Sir Walter Mildmay, Master Astley, and the rest said very little; only Sir Richard Sackville said nothing at all. After dinner I went up to read with the Queen's Majesty. We read then together in the Greek tongue, as I well remember, that noble oration of Demosthenes against Aeschines for his false dealing in his embassage to King Philip of Macedonia.[8] Sir Richard Sackville came up soon after, and, finding me in Her Majesty's privy chamber, he took me by the hand, and carrying me to a window, said:

Master Ascham, I would not for a good deal of money have been this day absent from dinner, where, though I said nothing, yet I gave as good ear and do consider as well the talk that passed as anyone did there. Master Secretary said very wisely, and most truly, that many young wits be driven to hate learning before they know what learning is. I can be good witness to this myself, for a fond schoolmaster, before I was fully fourteen year old, drave me so with

---

[7] Usually thought to be the playwright Nicholas Udall, who was headmaster of Eton from about 1534 to 1541. But since Ascham's response seems almost certainly intended as a compliment to Haddon, it is more likely that the person in question was Richard Cox, Bishop of Ely, who had been headmaster during Haddon's schooldays at Eton.

[8] Demosthenes, Περὶ τησ παραπρεσβείας (*On the False Embassy*).

fear of beating from all love of learning, as now when I know what difference it is to have learning and to have little or none at all, I feel it my greatest grief and find it my greatest hurt that ever came to me that it was my so ill chance to light upon so lewd a schoolmaster. But seeing it is but in vain to lament things past, and also wisdom to look to things to come, surely, God willing, if God lend me life I will make this my mishap some occasion of good hap to little Robert Sackville, my son's son. For whose bringing-up I would gladly, if it so please you, use specially your good advice. I hear say you have a son much of his age; we will deal thus together. Point you out a schoolmaster who, by your order, shall teach my son and yours, and for all the rest I will provide, yea, though they three do cost me a couple of hundred pounds by year; and beside, you shall find me as fast a friend to you and yours as perchance any you have.

Which promise the worthy gentleman surely kept with me until his dying day.

We had then further talk together of bringing-up of children: of the nature of quick and hard wits; of the right choice of a good wit; of fear and love in teaching children. We passed from children and came to young men, namely, gentlemen. We talked of their too much liberty to live as they lust; of their letting loose too soon to overmuch experience of ill, contrary to the good order of many good old commonwealths of the Persians and Greeks; of wit gathered and good fortune gotten by some only by experience, without learning. And lastly he required of me very earnestly to show what I thought of the common going of Englishmen into Italy. "But," saith he,

because this place and this time will not suffer so long talk as these good matters require, therefore I pray you, at my request and at your leisure, put in some order of writing the chief points of this our talk concerning the right order of teaching and honesty of living for the good bringing-up of children and young men. And surely, beside contenting me, you shall both please and profit very many others.

## A *Preface to the Reader*

I made some excuse by lack of ability and weakness of body. "Well," saith he,

I am not now to learn what you can do. Our dear friend, good Master Goodrich,[9] whose judgment I could well believe, did once for all satisfy me fully therein. Again, I heard you say not long ago that you may thank Sir John Cheke for all the learning you have. And I know very well myself that you did teach the Queen. And therefore, seeing God did so bless you to make you the scholar of the best master, and also the schoolmaster of the best scholar, that ever were in our time, surely you should please God, benefit your country, and honest [10] your own name, if you would take the pains to impart to others what you learned of such a master and how ye taught such a scholar. And in uttering the stuff ye received of the one, in declaring the order ye took with the other, ye shall never lack, neither matter nor manner, what to write nor how to write in this kind of argument.

I, beginning some farther excuse, suddenly was called to come to the Queen. The night following I slept little, my head was so full of this our former talk and I so mindful somewhat to satisfy the honest request of so dear a friend. I thought to prepare some little treatise for a New Year's gift that Christmas. But as it chanceth to busy builders, so in building this my poor schoolhouse (the rather because the form of it is somewhat new and differing from others) the work rose daily higher and wider than I thought it would at the beginning.

And though it appear now, and be in very deed, but a small cottage, poor for the stuff and rude for the workmanship, yet in going forward I found the site so good as I was loath to give it over, but the making so costly, outreaching my ability, as many times I wished that some one of those three, my dear friends

[9] Richard Goodrich, lawyer and member of various commissions appointed by Queen Elizabeth.
[10] Bring honor to.

*9*

with full purses, Sir Thomas Smith, Master Haddon, or Master Watson, had had the doing of it. Yet, nevertheless, I myself, spending gladly that little that I gat at home by good Sir John Cheke, and that that I borrowed abroad of my friend Sturmius, beside somewhat that was left me in reversion by my old masters, Plato, Aristotle, and Cicero, I have at last patched it up as I could and as you see. If the matter be mean and meanly handled, I pray you bear both with me and it, for never work went up in worse weather, with more lets and stops, than this poor schoolhouse of mine. Westminster Hall can bear some witness, beside much weakness of body, but more trouble of mind, by some such sores as grieve me to touch them myself, and therefore I purpose not to open them to others. And in midst of outward injuries and inward cares, to increase them withal, good Sir Richard Sackville dieth—that worthy gentleman, that earnest favorer and furtherer of God's true religion, that faithful servitor to his prince and country—a lover of learning and all learned men, wise in all doings, courteous to all persons, showing spite to none, doing good to many, and, as I well found, to me so fast a friend as I never lost the like before. When he was gone my heart was dead. There was not one that wore a black gown for him who carried a heavier heart for him than I. When he was gone I cast this book away; I could not look upon it but with weeping eyes in remembering him who was the only setter-on to do it and would have been, not only a glad commender of it, but also a sure and certain comfort to me and mine for it. Almost two years together this book lay scattered and neglected and had been quite given over of me, if the goodness of one had not given me some life and spirit again. God, the mover of goodness, prosper always him and his as he hath many times comforted me and mine, and, I trust to God, shall comfort more and more. Of whom most justly I may say, and very oft and always gladly I am wont to say, that sweet verse of Sophocles, spoken by Oedipus to worthy Theseus:

## A Preface to the Reader

Ἔχω, ἅ ἔχω, διὰ σὲ, κοὐκ ἄλλον βροτῶν.[11]

This hope hath helped me to end this book, which, if he allow, I shall think my labors well employed and shall not much esteem the misliking of any others. And I trust he shall think the better of it because he shall find the best part thereof to come out of his school whom he, of all men, loved and liked best.

Yet some men, friendly enough of nature but of small judgment in learning, do think I take too much pains and spend too much time in setting forth these children's affairs. But those good men were never brought up in Socrates' school, who saith plainly that no man goeth about a more godly purpose than he that is mindful of the good bringing-up both of his own and other men's children.[12]

Therefore I trust good and wise men will think well of this my doing. And of other that think otherwise, I will think myself they are but men, to be pardoned for their folly and pitied for their ignorance.

In writing this book, I have had earnest respect to three special points: truth of religion, honesty in living, right order in learning. In which three ways, I pray God, my poor children may diligently walk, for whose sake, as nature moved, and reason required, and necessity also somewhat compelled, I was the willinger to take these pains.

For seeing at my death I am not like to leave them any great store of living, therefore in my lifetime I thought good to bequeath unto them in this little book, as in my will and testament, the right way to good learning, which if they follow with the fear of God, they shall very well come to sufficiency of living.

I wish also with all my heart that young Master Robert

[11] Sophocles, *Oedipus at Colonus*, 1129: "For all I have I owe to thee alone." The compliment is directed to Cecil.

[12] Pseudo-Plato, *Theages*, 122B: Ὁν γὰρ ἔστι, περὶ ὅτου θειοτέρου ἄνθρωπος ἂν βουλεύσαιτο, ἢ περὶ παιδείας, καὶ τῶν αὑτοῦ, καὶ τῶν οἰκείων.

*11*

Sackville may take that fruit of this labor that his worthy grandfather purposed he should have done, and if any other do take either profit or pleasure hereby, they have cause to thank Master Robert Sackville, for whom specially this my *Schoolmaster* was provided.

And one thing I would have the reader consider in reading this book, that because no schoolmaster hath charge of any child before he enter into his school, therefore, I leaving all former care of their good bringing-up to wise and good parents as a matter not belonging to the schoolmaster, I do appoint this my schoolmaster then and there to begin where his office and charge beginneth. Which charge lasteth not long, but until the scholar be made able to go to the university, to proceed in logic, rhetoric, and other kinds of learning.

Yet if my schoolmaster, for love he beareth to his scholar, shall teach him somewhat for his furtherance and better judgment in learning that may serve him seven year after in the university, he doth his scholar no more wrong, nor deserveth no worse name thereby, than he doth in London who, selling silk or cloth unto his friend, doth give him better measure than either his promise or bargain was.

*Farewell in Christ.*

# The first book for the youth

AFTER the child hath learned perfectly the eight parts of speech, let him then learn the right joining together of substantives with adjectives, the noun with the verb, the relative with the antecedent. And in learning farther his *syntaxis*,[1] by mine advice he shall not use the common order in common schools for making of Latins, whereby the child commonly learneth, first, an evil choice of words (and right choice of words, saith Caesar, is the foundation of eloquence),[2] then, a wrong placing of words, and, lastly, an ill framing of the sentence, with a perverse judgment, both of words and sentences. These faults, taking once root in youth, be never or hardly plucked away in age. Moreover, there is no one thing that hath more either dulled the wits or taken away the will of children from learning than the care they have to satisfy their masters in making of Latins.

For the scholar is commonly beat for the making, when the master were more worthy to be beat for the mending, or rather,

---

[1] Proper choice of forms and arrangement of words in sentences.
[2] Cicero, *Brutus,* lxxii.253: *Verborum dilectum originem esse eloquentiae.*

**13**

marring of the same, the master many times being as ignorant as the child what to say properly and fitly to the matter.

Two schoolmasters have set forth in print either of them a book of such kind of Latins, Horman and Whittinton.[3]

A child shall learn of the better of them that which another day, if he be wise and come to judgment, he must be fain to unlearn again.

There is a way, touched in the first book of Cicero *De oratore*,[4] which, wisely brought into schools, truly taught, and constantly used, would not only take wholly away this butcherly fear in making of Latins but would also, with ease and pleasure and in short time, as I know by good experience, work a true choice and placing of words, a right ordering of sentences, an easy understanding of the tongue, a readiness to speak, a facility to write, a true judgment both of his own and other men's doings, what tongue soever he doth use.

The way is this. After the three concordances learned, as I touched before, let the master read unto him the epistles of Cicero gathered together and chosen out by Sturmius for the capacity of children.[5]

First let him teach the child, cheerfully and plainly, the cause and matter of the letter; then, let him construe it into English so oft as the child may easily carry away the understanding of it; lastly, parse it over perfectly. This done thus, let the child, by and by, both construe and parse it over again so that it may appear that the child doubteth in nothing that his master taught him before. After this, the child must take a paper book and, sitting in some place where no man shall prompt him, by

[3] The grammarians William Horman and Robert Whittinton, both of whom published *Vulgaria*, or phrase books, for use in Tudor schools. Horman's book appeared in 1519; Whittinton's, which was published in 1520, went through at least a dozen editions during the sixteenth century.

[4] *De oratore*, I.xxxiv.155.

[5] *Ciceronis epistolarum libri IV. a J. Sturmio puerili educatione confecti* (Strasbourg, 1539).

himself, let him translate into English his former lesson. Then, showing it to his master, let the master take from him his Latin book, and, pausing an hour at the least, then let the child translate his own English into Latin again in another paper book. When the child bringeth it turned into Latin, the master must compare it with Tully's [6] book and lay them both together, and where the child doth well, either in choosing or true placing of Tully's words, let the master praise him and say, "Here ye do well." For I assure you, there is no such whetstone to sharpen a good wit and encourage a will to learning as is praise.

But if the child miss, either in forgetting a word, or in changing a good with a worse, or misordering the sentence, I would not have the master either frown or chide with him, if the child have done his diligence and used no truantship therein. For I know by good experience that a child shall take more profit of two faults gently warned of than of four things rightly hit. For then the master shall have good occasion to say unto him:

N[omen], Tully would have used such a word, not this; Tully would have placed this word here, not there; would have used this case, this number, this person, this degree, this gender; he would have used this mood, this tense, this simple rather than this compound; this adverb here, not there; he would have ended the sentence with this verb, not with that noun or participle, etc.

In these few lines I have wrapped up the most tedious part of grammar and also the ground of almost all the rules that are so busily taught by the master, and so hardly learned by the scholar, in all common schools; which after this sort, the master shall teach without all error, and the scholar shall learn without great pain, the master being led by so sure a guide, and the scholar being brought into so plain and easy a way. And therefore we do not contemn rules, but we gladly teach rules, and

[6] Marcus Tullius Cicero.

teach them more plainly, sensibly, and orderly than they be commonly taught in common schools. For when the master shall compare Tully's book with his scholar's translation, let the master at the first lead and teach his scholar to join the rules of his grammar book with the examples of his present lesson, until the scholar by himself be able to fetch out of his grammar every rule for every example, so as the grammar book be ever in the scholar's hand and also used of him, as a dictionary, for every present use. This is a lively and perfect way of teaching of rules, where the common way, used in common schools, to read the grammar alone by itself, is tedious for the master, hard for the scholar, cold and uncomfortable for them both.

Let your scholar be never afraid to ask you any doubt, but use discreetly the best allurements ye can to encourage him to the same, lest his overmuch fearing of you drive him to seek some misorderly shift,[7] as to seek to be helped by some other book, or to be prompted by some other scholar, and so go about to beguile you much and himself more.

With this way—of good understanding the matter, plain construing, diligent parsing, daily translating, cheerful admonishing, and heedful amending of faults, never leaving behind just praise for well-doing—I would have the scholar brought up withal, till he had read and translated over the first book of epistles chosen out by Sturmius, with a good piece of a comedy of Terence also.

All this while, by mine advice, the child shall use to speak no Latin, for, as Cicero saith in like matter, with like words, *loquendo, male loqui discunt.*[8] And that excellent learned man Guillaume Budaeus, in his *Greek Commentaries*, sore complaineth that when he began to learn the Latin tongue, use of speaking Latin at the table and elsewhere unadvisedly did

[7] Subterfuge.

[8] "By speaking, they learn to speak badly." Cicero's actual words are: *Perverse dicere, homines, perverse dicendo, facillime consequi* (*De oratore,* I.xxxiii.150).

bring him to such an evil choice of words, to such a crooked framing of sentences, that no one thing did hurt or hinder him more all the days of his life afterward, both for readiness in speaking and also good judgment in writing.[9]

In very deed, if children were brought up in such a house, or such a school, where the Latin tongue were properly and perfectly spoken, as Tiberius and Caius Gracchi were brought up in their mother Cornelia's house, surely then the daily use of speaking were the best and readiest way to learn the Latin tongue. But now commonly, in the best schools in England, for words, right choice is smally regarded, true propriety wholly neglected; confusion is brought in, barbarousness is bred up so in young wits as afterward they be not only marred for speaking but also corrupted in judgment, as with much ado, or never at all, they be brought to right frame again.

Yet all men covet to have their children speak Latin, and so do I very earnestly too. We both have one purpose; we agree in desire, we wish one end; but we differ somewhat in order and way that leadeth rightly to that end. Other would have them speak at all adventures and, so they be speaking, to speak, the master careth not, the scholar knoweth not, what. This is to seem and not to be, except it be to be bold without shame, rash without skill, full of words without wit. I wish to have them speak so as it may well appear that the brain doth govern the tongue and that reason leadeth forth the talk. Socrates' doctrine is true in Plato,[10] and well marked and truly uttered by Horace in *Arte poetica*,[11] that wheresoever knowledge doth accompany the wit, there best utterance doth always await upon the

[9] Guillaume Budé, *Commentarii linguae Graecae* (Paris, 1529), p. 23.

[10] *Phaedrus*, 276A.

[11] "Of good writing the source and fount is wisdom. Your matter the Socratic pages can set forth, and when matter is in hand words will not be loath to follow" (ll. 309–311). Reprinted by permission of the publishers and the Loeb Classical Library from Horace, *Satires, Epistles, and Ars Poetica,* trans. H. Rushton Fairclough (Cambridge, Mass.: Harvard University Press, 1961), p. 477.

tongue. For good understanding must first be bred in the child, which, being nourished with skill and use of writing (as I will teach more largely hereafter), is the only way to bring him to judgment and readiness in speaking, and that in far shorter time (if he follow constantly the trade of this little lesson) than he shall do by common teaching of the common schools in England.

But to go forward: as you perceive your scholar to go better and better on away, first, with understanding his lesson more quickly, with parsing [12] more readily, with translating more speedily and perfectly than he was wont, after, give him longer lessons to translate, and, withal, begin to teach him, both in nouns and verbs, what is *proprium*, and what is *translatum*, what *synonymum*, what *diversum*, which be *contraria*, and which be most notable *phrases* in all his lecture.[13]

As:

| | |
|---|---|
| *Proprium* | $\left\{\right.$ *Rex sepultus est magnifice* |
| *Translatum* | $\left\{\begin{array}{l}\text{\textit{Cum illo principe, sepulta est et gloria}} \\ \text{\textit{et salus reipublicae}}\end{array}\right.$ |
| *Synonyma* | $\left\{\begin{array}{l}\text{\textit{Ensis, gladius}} \\ \text{\textit{Laudare, praedicare}}\end{array}\right.$ |
| *Diversa* | $\left\{\begin{array}{l}\text{\textit{Diligere, amare}} \\ \text{\textit{Calere, exardescere}} \\ \text{\textit{Inimicus, hostis}}\end{array}\right.$ |
| *Contraria* | $\left\{\begin{array}{l}\text{\textit{Acerbum et luctuosum bellum}} \\ \text{\textit{Dulcis et laeta pax}}\end{array}\right.$ |
| *Phrases* | $\left\{\begin{array}{l}\text{\textit{Dare verba}} \\ \text{\textit{Abjicere obedientiam.}}[14]\end{array}\right.$ |

[12] 1570: passing.      [13] Reading.

[14] Literal      $\left\{\right.$ The king was buried magnificently

18

## The Bringing-up of Youth

Your scholar then must have the third paper book, in the which, after he hath done his double translation, let him write after this sort four of these forenamed six, diligently marked out of every lesson.

$$
Quatuor \left\{ \begin{array}{l} Propria \\ Translata \\ Synonyma \\ Diversa \\ Contraria \\ Phrases. \end{array} \right.
$$

Or else three, or two, if there be no more, and if there be none of these at all in some lecture, yet not omit the order, but write these:

$$
\left\{ \begin{array}{l} Diversa\ nulla \\ Contraria\ nulla, etc. \end{array} \right.
$$

This diligent translating, joined with this heedful marking in the foresaid epistles and afterward in some plain oration of Tully, as *Pro lege Manilio, Pro Archia poeta,* or in those three *Ad Caium Caesarem,*[15] shall work such a right choice of words,

| Metaphorical | With that prince, both the glory and the security of the commonwealth is buried |
|---|---|
| Synonymous | A long sword, a short sword<br>Praise, commend |
| Slightly differing | Love from esteem, love from feeling<br>Be aroused, be violently excited<br>Private enemy, public foe |
| Opposite | Bitter and baleful war<br>Sweet and joyful peace |
| Expressions | Mislead<br>Cast off obedience. |

[15] The three orations are those in behalf of Quintus Ligarius, King Deiotarus, and Marcus Marcellus.

so straight a framing of sentences, such a true judgment, both to write skillfully and speak wittily, as wise men shall both praise and marvel at.

If your scholar do miss sometimes in marking rightly these foresaid six things, chide not hastily, for that shall both dull his wit and discourage his diligence; but monish [16] him gently, which shall make him both willing to amend and glad to go forward in love and hope of learning.

I have now wished, twice or thrice, this gentle nature to be in a schoolmaster, and that I have done so neither by chance nor without some reason I will now declare at large why, in mine opinion, love is fitter than fear, gentleness better than beating, to bring up a child rightly in learning.

With the common use of teaching and beating in common schools of England I will not greatly contend; which if I did, it were but a small grammatical controversy neither belonging to heresy nor treason nor greatly touching God nor the prince, although, in very deed, in the end the good or ill bringing-up of children doth as much serve to the good or ill service of God, our prince, and our whole country as any one thing doth beside.

I do gladly agree with all good schoolmasters in these points: to have children brought to good perfectness in learning, to all honesty in manners; to have all faults rightly amended; to have every vice severely corrected; but for the order and way that leadeth rightly to these points we somewhat differ. For commonly many schoolmasters, some, as I have seen, more, as I have heard tell, be of so crooked a nature as, when they meet with a hard-witted scholar, they rather break him than bow him, rather mar him than mend him. For when the schoolmaster is angry with some other matter, then will he soonest fall to beat his scholar, and though he himself should be punished for his folly, yet must he beat some scholar for his pleasure, though there be no cause for him to do so nor yet fault in the scholar to

[16] Admonish.

## The Bringing-up of Youth

deserve so. These, ye will say, be fond schoolmasters, and few they be that be found to be such. They be fond indeed, but surely overmany such be found everywhere. But this will I say, that even the wisest of your great beaters do as oft punish nature as they do correct faults. Yea, many times the better nature is sorer punished, for if one by quickness of wit take his lesson readily, another, by hardness of wit, taketh it not so speedily, the first is always commended, the other is commonly punished, when a wise schoolmaster should rather discreetly consider the right disposition of both their natures and not so much weigh what either of them is able to do now as what either of them is likely to do hereafter. For this I know, not only by reading of books in my study but also by experience of life abroad in the world, that those which be commonly the wisest, the best learned, and best men also, when they be old, were never commonly the quickest of wit when they were young. The causes why, amongst other, which be many, that move me thus to think, be these few which I will reckon. Quick wits commonly be apt to take, unapt to keep; soon hot and desirous of this and that, as cold and soon weary of the same again; more quick to enter speedily than able to pierce far, even like oversharp tools, whose edges be very soon turned. Such wits delight themselves in easy and pleasant studies and never pass far forward in high and hard sciences. And therefore the quickest wits commonly may prove the best poets but not the wisest orators—ready of tongue to speak boldly, not deep of judgment either for good counsel or wise writing. Also, for manners and life quick wits commonly be in desire newfangled, in purpose unconstant; light to promise anything, ready to forget everything, both benefit and injury, and thereby neither fast to friend nor fearful to foe; inquisitive of every trifle, not secret in greatest affairs; bold with any person, busy in every matter; soothing such as be present, nipping any that is absent; of nature, also, always flattering their betters, envying their equals, despising

21

their inferiors; and by quickness of wit very quick and ready to like none so well as themselves.

Moreover, commonly men very quick of wit be also very light of conditions and thereby very ready of disposition to be carried overquickly by any light company to any riot and unthriftiness when they be young, and therefore seldom either honest of life or rich in living when they be old. For quick in wit and light in manners be either seldom troubled or very soon weary in carrying a very heavy purse. Quick wits also be, in most part of all their doings, overquick, hasty, rash, heady, and brainsick. These two last words, *heady* and *brainsick*, be fit and proper words, rising naturally of the matter and termed aptly by the condition of overmuch quickness of wit. In youth also they be ready scoffers, privy mockers, and ever over light and merry. In age, soon testy, very waspish, and always overmiserable. And yet few of them come to any great age by reason of their misordered life when they were young, but a great deal fewer of them come to show any great countenance or bear any great authority abroad in the world, but either live obscurely, men know not how, or die obscurely, men mark not when. They be like trees that show forth fair blossoms and broad leaves in springtime, but bring out small and not long lasting fruit in harvest time, and that only such as fall and rot before they be ripe and so never, or seldom, come to any good at all. For this ye shall find most true by experience, that amongst a number of quick wits in youth, few be found, in the end, either very fortunate for themselves or very profitable to serve the commonwealth, but decay and vanish, men know not which way, except a very few to whom peradventure blood and happy parentage may perchance purchase a long standing upon the stage. The which felicity, because it cometh by others' procuring, not by their own deserving, and stand by other men's feet and not by their own, what outward brag [17] soever is borne by them is indeed, of itself and in wise men's eyes, of no great estimation.

[17] Swagger.

## The Bringing-up of Youth

Some wits, moderate enough by nature, be many times marred by overmuch study and use of some sciences, namely, music, arithmetic, and geometry. These sciences, as they sharpen men's wits overmuch, so they change men's manners oversore, if they be not moderately mingled and wisely applied to some good use of life. Mark all mathematical heads which be only and wholly bent to those sciences, how solitary they be themselves, how unfit to live with others, and how unapt to serve in the world. This is not only known now by common experience, but uttered long before by wise men's judgment and sentence. Galen saith, "Much music marreth men's manners," [18] and Plato hath a notable place of the same thing in his books *De republica,* well marked also and excellently translated by Tully himself.[19] Of this matter I wrote once more at large twenty year ago in my book of shooting.[20] Now I thought but to touch it, to prove that overmuch quickness of wit, either given by nature or sharpened by study, doth not commonly bring forth either greatest learning, best manners, or happiest life in the end.

Contrariwise, a wit in youth that is not overdull, heavy, knotty, and lumpish, but hard, rough, and though somewhat staffish—as Tully wisheth, *otium quietum, non languidum,* and *negotium cum labore, non cum periculo* [21]—such a wit, I say, if

---

[18] *Corrumpuntur animi mores priva consuetudine cujusque horum, cibi, potionis, exercitationis, videndi, audiendi, totius denique musices (De sanitate tuenda libri sex,* trans. Thomas Linacre [Tübingen, 1541], sig. C8r).

[19] Neither Plato nor Cicero says quite what Ascham implies. Plato is concerned rather with lawless and therefore harmful innovations in music (*Republic,* IV.424B–E), and Cicero, though he twice cites the same passage in his *De legibus* (II.xv.38–39, III.xiv.32), argues that it is not so much music that a society should worry about as changes in "the habits and mode of living of its aristocracy."

[20] *Toxophilus* (London, 1545), sig. C2r–v.

[21] "A quiet, not a dull leisure" and "occupation involving effort, but not risk." Cicero's actual phrase is: *in negotio sine periculo, vel in otio cum dignitate (De oratore,* I.i.1).

it be at first well handled by the mother and rightly smoothed and wrought as it should, not overthwartly and against the wood, by the schoolmaster, both for learning and whole course of living proveth always the best. In wood and stone, not the softest, but hardest, be always aptest for portraiture, both fairest for pleasure and most durable for profit. Hard wits be hard to receive but sure to keep, painful without weariness, heedful without wavering, constant without newfangledness; bearing heavy things, though not lightly, yet willingly; entering hard things, though not easily, yet deeply; and so come to that perfectness of learning in the end that quick wits seem in hope, but do not in deed, or else very seldom, ever attain unto. Also, for manners and life hard wits commonly are hardly carried either to desire every new thing or else to marvel at every strange thing, and therefore they be careful and diligent in their own matters, not curious and busy in other men's affairs; and so they become wise themselves and also are counted honest by others. They be grave, steadfast, silent of tongue, secret of heart; not hasty in making, but constant in keeping, any promise; not rash in uttering, but ware in considering, every matter, and thereby not quick in speaking, but deep of judgment, whether they write or give counsel, in all weighty affairs. And these be the men that become in the end both most happy for themselves and always best esteemed abroad in the world.

I have been longer in describing the nature, the good or ill success, of the quick and hard wit than perchance some will think this place and matter doth require. But my purpose was hereby plainly to utter what injury is offered to all learning and to the commonwealth also, first, by the fond father in choosing but, chiefly, by the lewd schoolmaster in beating and driving away the best natures from learning. A child that is still, silent, constant, and somewhat hard of wit is either never chosen by the father to be made a scholar, or else, when he cometh to the school, he is smally regarded, little looked unto. He lacketh teaching, he lacketh couraging, he lacketh all things; only he never lacketh beating, nor any word that may move him to hate learning, nor any deed that may drive him from learning to any other kind of living.

And when this sad-natured [22] and hard-witted child is beat from his book and becometh after either student of the common law, or page in the court, or servingman, or bound prentice to a merchant or to some handicraft, he proveth in the end wiser, happier, and many times honester, too, than many of these quick wits do by their learning.

Learning is both hindered and injured too by the ill choice of them that send young scholars to the universities, of whom needs must come all our divines, lawyers, and physicians.

These young scholars be chosen commonly as young apples be chosen by children in a fair garden about St. James's tide.[23] A child will choose a sweeting [24] because it is presently fair and pleasant, and refuse a rennet [25] because it is then green, hard, and sour, when the one if it be eaten doth breed both worms and ill humors, the other if it stand his [26] time, be ordered and kept as it should, is wholesome of itself and helpeth to the good digestion of other meats. Sweetings will receive worms, rot and die on the tree, and never or seldom come to the gathering for good and lasting store.

For very grief of heart I will not apply the similitude, but hereby is plainly seen how learning is robbed of her best wits, first, by the great beating and, after, by the ill choosing of scholars to go to the universities. Whereof cometh partly that lewd and spiteful proverb, sounding to the great hurt of learning and shame of learned men, that "the greatest clerks [27] be not the wisest men."

And though I, in all this discourse, seem plainly to prefer hard and rough wits before quick and light wits both for

[22] Serious.      [23] July 25.      [24] An early-ripening, very sweet apple.
[25] A late-ripening pippin.      [26] Its.      [27] Scholars.

learning and manners, yet am I not ignorant that some quickness of wit is a singular gift of God, and so most rare amongst men, and namely such a wit as is quick without lightness, sharp without brittleness, desirous of good things without newfangledness, diligent in painful things without wearisomeness, and constant in good will to do all things well, as I know was in Sir John Cheke, and is in some that yet live, in whom all these fair qualities of wit are fully met together.

But it is notable and true that Socrates saith in Plato to his friend Crito: that that number of men is fewest which far exceed, either in good or ill, in wisdom or folly, but the mean betwixt both be the greatest number; which he proveth true in diverse other things, as in greyhounds, amongst which few are found exceeding great or exceeding little, exceeding swift or exceeding slow.[28] And therefore, I speaking of quick and hard wits, I meant the common number of quick and hard wits, amongst the which for the most part the hard wit proveth many times the better learned, wiser, and honester man, and therefore do I the more lament that such wits commonly be either kept from learning by fond fathers or beat from learning by lewd schoolmasters.

And speaking thus much of the wits of children for learning, the opportunity of the place and goodness of the matter might require to have here declared the most special notes of a good wit for learning in a child, after the manner and custom of a good horseman who is skillful to know and able to tell others how, by certain sure signs, a man may choose a colt that is like to prove another day excellent for the saddle. And it is pity that commonly more care is had, yea, and that amongst very wise men, to find out rather a cunning man for their horse than a

---

[28] Plato, *Phaedo,* 89E–90A, where Socrates asks, "Have you not noticed that the extremes in all these instances are rare and few, and the examples between the extremes are very many?" Marginal note mistakenly cites the *Crito.*

cunning man for their children. They say nay in word, but they do so in deed. For to the one they will gladly give a stipend of two hundred crowns by year and loathe to offer the other two hundred shillings. God that sitteth in heaven laugheth their choice to scorn and rewardeth their liberality as it should, for he suffereth them to have tame and well-ordered horse but wild and unfortunate children; and therefore in the end they find more pleasure in their horse than comfort in their children.

But concerning the true notes of the best wits for learning in a child, I will report, not mine own opinion, but the very judgment of him that was counted the best teacher and wisest man that learning maketh mention of, and that is Socrates in Plato, who expresseth orderly these seven plain notes to choose a good wit in a child for learning:

1. 'Ευφυής
2. Μνήμων
3. Φιλομαθής
4. Φιλόπονος
5. Φιλήκοος
6. Ζητητικός
7. Φιλέπαινος.[29]

And because I write English, and to Englishmen, I will plainly declare in English both what these words of Plato mean, and how aptly they be linked, and how orderly they follow one another.

### 1. 'Ευφυής

Is he that is apt by goodness of wit and appliable by readiness of will to learning, having all other qualities of the mind and parts of the body that must another day serve learning, not troubled, mangled, and halved, but sound, whole, full, and able

[29] Plato, *Republic*, VII.535B–D. Only points two through six appear in this passage. The first, ευφυής, occurs in *Republic*, V.455B; for the last, φιλέπαινος, I can find no source in Plato.

27

to do their office, as: a tongue not stammering or overhardly drawing forth words, but plain and ready to deliver the meaning of the mind; a voice not soft, weak, piping, womanish, but audible, strong, and manlike; a countenance not wearish [30] and crabbed but fair and comely; a personage not wretched and deformed but tall and goodly; for surely a comely countenance with a goodly stature giveth credit to learning and authority to the person; otherwise commonly either open contempt or privy disfavor doth hurt or hinder both person and learning. And even as a fair stone requireth to be set in the finest gold with the best workmanship, or else it loseth much of the grace and price, even so excellency in learning, and namely divinity, joined with a comely personage, is a marvelous jewel in the world. And how can a comely body be better employed than to serve the fairest exercise of God's greatest gift, and that is learning. But commonly the fairest bodies are bestowed on the foulest purposes. I would it were not so, and with examples herein I will not meddle; yet I wish that those should mind it and meddle with it which have most occasion to look to it, as good and wise fathers should do, and greatest authority to amend it, as good and wise magistrates ought to do; and yet I will not let [31] openly to lament the unfortunate case of learning herein.

For if a father have four sons, three fair and well formed both mind and body, the fourth wretched, lame, and deformed, his choice shall be to put the worst to learning as one good enough to become a scholar. I have spent the most part of my life in the university, and therefore I can bear good witness that many fathers commonly do thus, whereof I have heard many wise, learned, and as good men as ever I knew make great and oft complaint: "A good horseman will choose no such colt, neither for his own, nor yet for his master's saddle." And thus much of the first note.

[30] Sickly-looking.    [31] Omit.

## The Bringing-up of Youth

### 2. Μνήμων

Good of memory, a special part of the first note εὐφυής, and a mere benefit of nature; yet it is so necessary for learning as Plato maketh it a separate and perfect note of itself, and that so principal a note as without it all other gifts of nature do small service to learning. Afranius, that old Latin poet, maketh memory the mother of learning and wisdom, saying thus: *Usus me genuit, mater peperit Memoria,*[32] and though it be the mere gift of nature, yet is memory well preserved by use and much increased by order, as our scholar must learn another day in the university, but in a child a good memory is well known by three properties; that is, if it be quick in receiving, sure in keeping, and ready in delivering forth again.

### 3. Φιλομαθής

Given to love learning; for though a child have all the gifts of nature at wish and perfection of memory at will, yet if he have not a special love to learning, he shall never attain to much learning. And therefore Isocrates, one of the noblest schoolmasters that is in memory of learning, who taught kings and princes, as Halicarnasseus writeth,[33] and out of whose school, as Tully saith, came forth more noble captains, more wise counselors, than did out of Epeius' horse at Troy [34]—this Isocrates, I say, did cause to be written at the entry of his school, in golden letters, this golden sentence: Ἐὰν ἦς φιλομαθής, ἔση πολυμαθής, which, excellently said in Greek, is thus rudely in English: "If thou lovest learning, thou shalt attain to much learning." [35]

[32] Aulus Gellius, *The Attic Nights,* XIII.viii.3: "My sire Experience was, me Memory bore."

[33] Dionysius Halicarnasseus, Ἰσοκράτους βίος, prefixed to *Isocrates nuper accurate recognitus, et auctus* (Venice, 1534), sig. A4r–v.

[34] *De oratore,* II.xxii.94: *Ecce tibi exortus est Isocrates, magister rhetorum omnium, cujus e ludo, tanquam ex equo Troiano, meri principes exierunt; sed eorum partim in acie illustres esse voluerunt.*

[35] *To Demonicus,* 18.

# The Schoolmaster

## 4. Φιλόπονος

Is he that hath a lust to labor and a will to take pains. For if a child have all the benefits of nature, with perfection of memory, love, like, and praise learning never so much, yet if he be not of himself painful, he shall never attain unto it. And yet where love is present labor is seldom absent, and namely in study of learning and matters of the mind. And therefore did Isocrates rightly judge that if his scholar were φιλομαθής, he cared for no more. Aristotle, varying from Isocrates in private affairs of life but agreeing with Isocrates in common judgment of learning, for love and labor in learning is of the same opinion, uttered in these words in his *Rhetoric ad Theodecten:* "Liberty kindleth love; love refuseth no labor; and labor obtaineth whatsoever it seeketh." [36] And yet, nevertheless, goodness of nature may do little good, perfection of memory may serve to small use, all love may be employed in vain, any labor may be soon graveled, [37] if a man trust always to his own singular wit and will not be glad sometime to hear, take advice, and learn of another. And therefore doth Socrates very notably add the fifth note:

## 5. Φιλήκοος

He that is glad to hear and learn of another. For otherwise he shall stick with great trouble where he might go easily forward, and also catch hardly a very little by his own toil when he might gather quickly a good deal by another man's teaching. But now there be some that have great love to learning, good lust to labor, be willing to learn of others, yet either of a fond shamefastness, or else of a proud folly, they dare not, or will not, go to learn of another. And therefore doth Socrates wisely add the sixth note of a good wit in a child for learning, and that is

[36] No exact parallel to these words occurs in Aristotle's *Rhetoric.* Ascham may have in mind a similar idea appearing in II.1392B, a discussion of how to establish whether a thing has or has not happened.

[37] Brought to no effect.

## The Bringing-up of Youth

### 6. Ζητητικός

He that is naturally bold to ask any question, desirous to search out any doubt, not ashamed to learn of the meanest, not afraid to go to the greatest, until he be perfectly taught and fully satisfied. The seventh and last point is

### 7. Φιλέπαινος

He that loveth to be praised for well-doing at his father's or master's hand. A child of this nature will earnestly love learning, gladly labor for learning, willingly learn of other, boldly ask any doubt. And thus, by Socrates' judgment, a good father and a wise schoolmaster should choose a child to make a scholar of that hath by nature the foresaid perfect qualities and comely furniture, both of mind and body; hath memory quick to receive, sure to keep, and ready to deliver; hath love to learning; hath lust to labor; hath desire to learn of others; hath boldness to ask any question; hath mind wholly bent to win praise by well-doing.

The two first points be special benefits of nature which nevertheless be well preserved and much increased by good order. But as for the five last, love, labor, gladness to learn of others, boldness to ask doubts, and will to win praise be won and maintained by the only wisdom and discretion of the schoolmaster. Which five points, whether a schoolmaster shall work sooner in a child by fearful beating or courteous handling, you that be wise judge.

Yet some men, wise indeed but in this matter, more by severity of nature than any wisdom at all, do laugh at us when we thus wish and reason that young children should rather be allured to learning by gentleness and love than compelled to learning by beating and fear. They say our "reasons serve only to breed forth talk and pass away time, but we never saw schoolmaster do so, nor never read of wise man that thought so."

## The Schoolmaster

Yes, forsooth, as wise as they be, either in other men's opinion or in their own conceit, I will bring the contrary judgment of him who, they themselves shall confess, was as wise as they are, or else they may be justly thought to have small wit at all; and that is Socrates, whose judgment in Plato is plainly this in these words (which, because they be very notable, I will recite them in his own tongue): Ὀυδὲν μάθημα μετὰ δουλείας χρὴ μανθάνειν· οἱ μὲν γὰρ τοῦ σώματος πόνοι βίᾳ πονούμενοι χεῖρον οὐδὲν τὸ σῶμα ἀπεργάζονται, ψυχῇ δὲ βίαιον οὐδὲν ἔμμονον μάθημα.[38] In English thus: "No learning ought to be learned with bondage, for bodily labors wrought by compulsion hurt not the body, but any learning learned by compulsion tarrieth not long in the mind." And why? For whatsoever the mind doth learn unwillingly with fear, the same it doth quickly forget without care. And lest proud wits, that love not to be contraried but have lust to wrangle or trifle away truth, will say that Socrates meaneth not this of children's teaching, but of some other higher learning, hear what Socrates in the same place doth more plainly say: Μὴ τοίνυν βίᾳ, ὦ ἄριστε, τοὺς παῖδας ἐν τοῖς μαθήμασιν ἀλλὰ παίζοντας τρέφε; that is to say, "And therefore, my dear friend, bring not up your children in learning by compulsion and fear, but by playing and pleasure." And you that do read Plato as ye should do well perceive that these be no questions asked by Socrates as doubts, but they be sentences, first affirmed by Socrates as mere truths, and after given forth by Socrates as right rules, most necessary to be marked and fit to be followed of all them that would have children taught as they should. And in this counsel, judgment, and authority of Socrates I will repose myself until I meet with a man of the contrary mind whom I may justly take to be wiser than I think Socrates was. Fond schoolmasters neither can understand nor will follow this good counsel of Socrates, but wise riders, in their office, can and will do both; which is the only cause that commonly the young gentlemen of England go

[38] Plato, *Republic*, VII.536E.

so unwillingly to school and run so fast to the stable. For in very deed fond schoolmasters, by fear, do beat into them the hatred of learning, and wise riders, by gentle allurements, do breed up in them the love of riding. They find fear and bondage in schools; they feel liberty and freedom in stables; which causeth them utterly to abhor the one and most gladly to haunt the other. And I do not write this that, in exhorting to the one, I would dissuade young gentlemen from the other. Yea, I am sorry with all my heart that they be given no more to riding than they be, for of all outward qualities, to ride fair is most comely for himself, most necessary for his country, and the greater he is in blood, the greater is his praise, the more he doth exceed all other therein. It was one of the three excellent praises amongst the noble gentlemen the old Persians: always to say truth, to ride fair, and shoot well; and so it was engraven upon Darius' tomb, as Strabo beareth witness:

> Darius the king lieth buried here,
> Who in riding and shooting had never peer.[39]

But to our purpose. Young men, by any means losing the love of learning, when by time they come to their own rule, they carry commonly from the school with them a perpetual hatred of their master and a continual contempt of learning. If ten gentlemen be asked why they forget so soon in court that which they were learning so long in school, eight of them, or let me be blamed, will lay the fault on their ill-handling by their schoolmasters.

Cuspinian doth report that that noble Emperor Maximilian would lament very oft his misfortune herein.[40]

Yet some will say that children of nature love pastime and mislike learning because, in their kind,[41] the one is easy and

[39] Strabo, XV.iii.8.
[40] Joannes Cuspinianus, *De Caesaribus atque imperatoribus Romanis, opus insigne* (Basel, 1561), pp. 602–603.
[41] Nature.

pleasant, the other hard and wearisome; which is an opinion not so true as some men ween. For the matter lieth not so much in the disposition of them that be young as in the order and manner of bringing-up by them that be old, nor yet in the difference of learning and pastime. For beat a child if he dance not well and cherish him though he learn not well, ye shall have him unwilling to go to dance and glad to go to his book. Knock him always when he draweth his shaft ill and favor him again though he fault at his book, ye shall have him very loath to be in the field and very willing to be in the school. Yea, I say more, and not of myself but by the judgment of those from whom few wise men will gladly dissent, that if ever the nature of man be given at any time more than other to receive goodness, it is in innocency of young years before that experience of evil have taken root in him. For the pure clean wit of a sweet young babe is, like the newest wax, most able to receive the best and fairest printing and, like a new bright silver dish never occupied, to receive and keep clean any good thing that is put into it.

And thus will in children, wisely wrought withal, may easily be won to be very willing to learn. And wit in children by nature, namely memory, the only key and keeper of all learning, is readiest to receive and surest to keep any manner of thing that is learned in youth; this, lewd and learned, by common experience, know to be most true. For we remember nothing so well when we be old as those things which we learned when we were young, and this is not strange but common in all nature's works. Every man sees (as I said before) new wax is best for printing, new clay fittest for working, new shorn wool aptest for soon and surest dyeing, new fresh flesh for good and durable salting. And this similitude is not rude, nor borrowed of the larder house, but out of his schoolhouse of whom the wisest in England need not be ashamed to learn. Young grafts grow not only soonest but also fairest, and bring always forth the best and sweetest fruit; young whelps learn easily to carry; young popinjays learn quickly to speak—and so, to be short, if in all other things, though they lack reason, sense, and life, the similitude of youth is fittest to all goodness, surely nature in mankind is most beneficial and effectual in this behalf.

Therefore, if to the goodness of nature be joined the wisdom of the teacher in leading young wits into a right and plain way of learning, surely children, kept up in God's fear and governed by his grace, may most easily be brought well to serve God and country both by virtue and wisdom.

But if will and wit, by farther age, be once allured from innocency, delighted in vain sights, filed [42] with foul talk, crooked with willfulness, hardened with stubbornness, and let loose to disobedience, surely it is hard with gentleness, but unpossible with severe cruelty, to call them back to good frame again. For where the one perchance may bend it, the other shall surely break it, and so instead of some hope leave an assured desperation and shameless contempt of all goodness, the farthest point in all mischief, as Xenophon doth most truly and most wittily mark. [43]

Therefore, to love or to hate, to like or contemn, to ply this way or that way to good or to bad, ye shall have as ye use a child in his youth.

And one example, whether love or fear doth work more in a child for virtue and learning, I will gladly report; which may be heard with some pleasure and followed with more profit. Before I went into Germany, I came to Broadgate in Leicestershire to take my leave of that noble Lady Jane Grey, to whom I was exceeding much beholding. Her parents, the duke and the duchess, with all the household, gentlemen and gentlewomen, were hunting in the park. I found her in her chamber reading

[42] Defiled; 1571: filled.
[43] *Cyropaedia*, I.ii.7: "For it seems that shamelessness goes hand in hand with ingratitude; and it is that, we know, which leads the way to every moral wrong."

# The Schoolmaster

*Phaedon Platonis* in Greek, and that with as much delight as some gentleman would read a merry tale in Boccaccio. After salutation and duty done, with some other talk, I asked her why she would lose such pastime in the park. Smiling she answered me, "Iwis,[44] all their sport in the park is but a shadow to that pleasure that I find in Plato. Alas, good folk, they never felt what true pleasure meant." "And how came you, madame," quoth I, "to this deep knowledge of pleasure, and what did chiefly allure you unto it, seeing not many women, but very few men, have attained thereunto?" "I will tell you," quoth she, "and tell you a truth which perchance ye will marvel at. One of the greatest benefits that ever God gave me is that he sent me so sharp and severe parents and so gentle a schoolmaster. For when I am in presence either of father or mother, whether I speak, keep silence, sit, stand, or go, eat, drink, be merry or sad, be sewing, playing, dancing, or doing anything else, I must do it, as it were, in such weight, measure, and number, even so perfectly as God made the world, or else I am so sharply taunted, so cruelly threatened, yea, presently sometimes, with pinches, nips, and bobs, and other ways which I will not name for the honor I bear them, so without measure misordered, that I think myself in hell till time come that I must go to Master Aylmer, who teacheth me so gently, so pleasantly, with such fair allurements to learning, that I think all the time nothing whilst I am with him. And when I am called from him, I fall on weeping because whatsoever I do else but learning is full of grief, trouble, fear, and whole misliking unto me. And thus my book hath been so much my pleasure, and bringeth daily to me more pleasure and more, that in respect of it all other pleasures in very deed be but trifles and troubles unto me." I remember this talk gladly, both because it is so worthy of memory and because also it was the last talk that ever I had, and the last time that ever I saw, that noble and worthy lady.

[44] Truly.

## The Bringing-up of Youth

I could be overlong, both in showing just causes and in reciting true examples, why learning should be taught rather by love than fear. He that would see a perfect discourse of it, let him read that learned treatise which my friend Joannes Sturmius wrote *De institutione principis* to the Duke of Cleves.[45]

The godly counsels of Solomon and Jesus, the son of Sirach, for sharp keeping-in and bridling of youth [46] are meant rather for fatherly correction than masterly beating, rather for manners than for learning, for other places than for schools. For God forbid but all evil touches, wantonness, lying, picking,[47] sloth, will, stubbornness, and disobedience should be with sharp chastisement daily cut away.

This discipline was well known and diligently used among the Grecians and old Romans, as doth appear in Aristophanes, Isocrates, and Plato, and also in the comedies of Plautus, where we see that children were under the rule of three persons: *praeceptore, paedagogo, parente.* The schoolmaster taught him learning with all gentleness; the governor corrected his manners with much sharpness; the father held the stern of his whole obedience. And so he that used to teach did not commonly use to beat but remitted that over to another man's charge. But what shall we say when now in our days the schoolmaster is used both for *praeceptor* in learning and *paedagogus* in manners? Surely, I would he should not confound their offices but discreetly use the duty of both so that neither ill touches should be left unpunished nor gentleness in teaching any wise omitted. And he shall well do both if wisely he do appoint diversity of

[45] This work of Sturm was printed with Conrad Heresbach, *De laudibus Graecarum literarum oratio* (Strasbourg, 1551); also included is an exchange of epistles between Ascham and Sturm *De nobilitate Anglicana.*

[46] Marginal note: *Qui parcit virgae, odit filium.* From Prov. 13:24: "He that spareth the rod hateth his son." Compare Ecclus. (Jesus, the son of Sirach) 30:1: "He that loveth his son will continue to lay strokes upon him."

[47] Pilfering.

time and separate place for either purpose, using always such discreet moderation as the schoolhouse should be counted a sanctuary against fear, and very well learning a common pardon for ill-doing, if the fault of itself be not overheinous.

And thus the children, kept up in God's fear and preserved by his grace, finding pain in ill-doing and pleasure in well studying, should easily be brought to honesty of life and perfectness of learning, the only mark that good and wise fathers do wish and labor that their children should most busily and carefully shoot at.

There is another discommodity, besides cruelty in schoolmasters in beating away the love of learning from children, which hindereth learning and virtue and good bringing-up of youth, and namely young gentlemen, very much in England. This fault is clean contrary to the first. I wished before to have love of learning bred up in children; I wish as much now to have young men brought up in good order of living and in some more severe discipline than commonly they be. We have lack in England of such good order as the old noble Persians so carefully used, whose children to the age of twenty-one year were brought up in learning and exercises of labor, and that in such place where they should neither see that was uncomely nor hear that was unhonest.[48] Yea, a young gentleman was never free to go where he would and do what he list himself, but under the keep and by the counsel of some grave governor, until he was either married or called to bear some office in the commonwealth.

And see the great obedience that was used in old time to fathers and governors. No son, were he never so old of years, never so great of birth, though he were a king's son, might not marry but by his father's, and mother's also, consent. Cyrus the

[48] Xenophon, *Cyropaedia*, VII.v.86: "The boys could not easily turn out bad, even if they should wish to, if they neither see nor hear anything vicious but spend their days in good and noble pursuits."

## The Bringing-up of Youth

Great, after he had conquered Babylon and subdued rich King Croesus with whole Asia Minor, coming triumphantly home, his uncle Cyaxares offered him his daughter to wife. Cyrus thanked his uncle and praised the maid, but for marriage he answered him with these wise and sweet words, as they be uttered by Xenophon: Ὦ κυαξάρη, τό τε γένος απαινῶ καὶ τὴν παῖδα καὶ τὰ δῶρα· βούλομαι δέ, ἔφη, σὺν τῇ τοῦ πατρὸς γνώμῃ καὶ τῆς μητρὸς ταῦτά σοι συναινέσαι, etc.[49] That is to say: "Uncle Cyaxares, I commend the stock, I like the maid, and I allow well the dowry, but (saith he) by the counsel and consent of my father and mother I will determine farther of these matters."

Strong Samson also, in Scripture, saw a maid that liked [50] him, but he spake not to her, but went home to his father and his mother and desired both father and mother to make the marriage for him. Doth this modesty, doth this obedience that was in great King Cyrus and stout Samson remain in our young men at this day? No, surely, for we live not longer after them by time than we live far different from them by good order. Our time is so far from that old discipline and obedience as now not only young gentlemen, but even very girls, dare without all fear, though not without open shame, where they list, and how they list, marry themselves in spite of father, mother, God, good order, and all. The cause of this evil is that youth is least looked unto when they stand most need of good keep and regard. It availeth not to see them well taught in young years and after, when they come to lust and youthful days, to give them license to live as they lust themselves. For if we suffer the eye of a young gentleman once to be entangled with vain sights, and the ear to be corrupted with fond or filthy talk, the mind shall quickly fall sick and soon vomit and cast up all the wholesome doctrine that he received in childhood, though he were never so well brought up before. And being once englutted with vanity,

[49] *Ibid.*, VIII.v.20.      [50] Pleased.

he will straightway loathe all learning and all good counsel to the same. And the parents, for all their great cost and charge, reap only in the end the fruit of grief and care.

This evil is not common to poor men, as God will have it, but proper to rich and great men's children, as they deserve it. Indeed from seven to seventeen young gentlemen commonly be carefully enough brought up, but from seventeen to seven-and-twenty (the most dangerous time of all a man's life and most slippery to stay well in) they have commonly the rein of all license in their own hand, and specially such as do live in the court. And that which is most to be marveled at, commonly the wisest and also best men be found the fondest fathers in this behalf. And if some good father would seek some remedy herein, yet the mother (if the house hold of our lady) had rather, yea, and will, too, have her son cunning and bold in making him to live trimly [51] when he is young, than by learning and travail to be able to serve his prince and country both wisely in peace and stoutly in war when he is old.

The fault is in yourselves, ye noblemen's sons, and therefore ye deserve the greater blame that commonly the meaner men's children come to be the wisest counselors and greatest doers in the weighty affairs of this realm. And why? For God will have it so of his providence because ye will have it no otherwise by your negligence.

And God is a good God, and wisest in all his doings, that will place virtue and displace vice in those kingdoms where he doth govern. For he knoweth that nobility without virtue and wisdom is blood indeed but blood, truly, without bones and sinews, and so of itself, without the other, very weak to bear the burden of weighty affairs.

The greatest ship indeed commonly carrieth the greatest burden, but yet always with the greatest jeopardy, not only for the

[51] Elegantly.

persons and goods committed unto it, but even for the ship itself, except it be governed with the greater wisdom.

But nobility governed by learning and wisdom is indeed most like a fair ship, having tide and wind at will, under the rule of a skillful master, when contrariwise a ship carried, yea, with the highest tide and greatest wind, lacking a skillful master, most commonly doth either sink itself upon sands or break itself upon rocks. And even so, how many have been either drowned in vain pleasure or overwhelmed by stout willfulness, the histories of England be able to afford overmany examples unto us. Therefore, ye great and noble men's children, if ye will have rightfully that praise and enjoy surely that place which your fathers have, and elders had and left unto you, ye must keep it as they gat it, and that is by the only way of virtue, wisdom, and worthiness.

For wisdom and virtue there be many fair examples in this court for young gentlemen to follow. But they be like fair marks in the field, out of a man's reach, too far off to shoot at well. The best and worthiest men, indeed, be sometimes seen but seldom talked withal; a young gentleman may sometime kneel to their person, smally use their company for their better instruction.

But young gentlemen are fain commonly to do in the court as young archers do in the field; that is, take such marks as be nigh them, although they be never so foul to shoot at. I mean, they be driven to keep company with the worst, and what force ill company hath to corrupt good wits the wisest men know best.

And not ill company only, but the ill opinion also of the most part, doth much harm, and namely of those which should be wise in the true deciphering of the good disposition of nature, of comeliness in courtly manners, and all right doings of men.

But error and fantasy do commonly occupy the place of truth and judgment. For if a young gentleman be demure and still of nature, they say he is simple and lacketh wit; if he be bashful and will soon blush, they call him a babyish and ill-brought-up thing, when Xenophon doth precisely note in Cyrus that his bashfulness in youth was the very true sign of his virtue and stoutness after; [52] if he be innocent and ignorant of ill, they say he is rude and hath no grace, so ungraciously do some graceless men misuse the fair and godly word GRACE.

But if ye would know what grace they mean, go, and look, and learn amongst them, and ye shall see that it is, first, to blush at nothing. And blushing in youth, saith Aristotle, is nothing else but fear to do ill,[53] which fear being once lustily frayed away from youth, then followeth to dare do any mischief, to contemn stoutly any goodness, to be busy in every matter, to be skillful in everything, to acknowledge no ignorance at all. To do thus in court is counted of some the chief and greatest grace of all and termed by the name of a virtue, called courage and boldness, when Crassus in Cicero teacheth the clean contrary, and that most wittily, saying thus: *Audere, cum bonis etiam rebus conjunctum, per se ipsum est magnopere fugiendum.*[54] Which is to say, "To be bold, yea, in a good matter, is for itself greatly to be eschewed."

Moreover, where the swing goeth, there to follow, fawn, flatter, laugh, and lie lustily at other men's liking. To face, stand foremost, shove back, and, to the meaner man or unknown in the court, to seem somewhat solemn, coy, big, and dangerous of look, talk, and answer; to think well of himself, to be lusty in contemning of others, to have some trim grace in a privy mock. And in greater presence to bear a brave look; to be warlike, though he never looked enemy in the face in war; yet some warlike sign must be used, either a slovenly busking [55] or an overstaring frounced [56] head, as though out of every hair's

[52] Xenophon, *Cyropaedia,* I.iv.4.
[53] *Nicomachean Ethics,* IV.ix.3: "We think it proper for the young to be modest, because as they live by feeling they often err, and modesty may keep them in check. . . ."
[54] *De oratore,* III.xxiv.94.    [55] Attire; headdress.
[56] Angry-looking, or, possibly, frizzed.

42

top should suddenly start out a good big oath when need requireth. Yet praised be God, England hath at this time many worthy captains and good soldiers which be indeed so honest of behavior, so comely of conditions, so mild of manners, as they may be examples of good order to a good sort of others which never came in war. But to return where I left. In place, also, to be able to raise talk and make discourse of every rush; [57] to have a very good will to hear himself speak; to be seen in palmistry, whereby to convey to chaste ears some fond or filthy talk.

And if some Smithfield [58] ruffian take up some strange going,[59] some new mowing [60] with the mouth, some wrenching with the shoulder, some brave proverb, some fresh new oath that is not stale but will run round in the mouth, some new disguised garment or desperate hat, fond in fashion or garish in color, whatsoever it cost, how small soever his living be, by what shift soever it be gotten, gotten must it be and used with the first, or else the grace of it is stale and gone. Some part of this graceless grace was described by me in a little rude verse long ago:

> To laugh, to lie, to flatter, to face,
> Four ways in court to win men grace.
> If thou be thrall to none of these,
> Away, good peak-goose,[61] hence, John Cheese!
> Mark well my word, and mark their deed,
> And think this verse part of thy creed.

Would to God this talk were not true and that some men's doings were not thus. I write not to hurt any, but to profit some; to accuse none, but monish such who, allured by ill counsel and following ill example, contrary to their good bringing-up and against their own good nature, yield overmuch to these follies and faults. I know many servingmen of good order and well staid, and again I hear say there be some servingmen do but ill

---

[57] Trifling thing.   [58] A tough market district of London.
[59] Manner of walking.   [60] Grimace.   [61] Simpleton.

service to their young masters. Yea, read Terence and Plautus advisedly over and ye shall find in those two wise writers, almost in every comedy, no unthrifty young man that is not brought thereunto by the subtle enticement of some lewd servant. And even now in our days Getae and Davi, Gnathos and many bold, bawdy Phormios, too, be pressing in to prattle on every stage, to meddle in every matter, when honest Parmenos [62] shall not be heard, but bear small swing with their masters. Their company, their talk, their overgreat experience in mischief doth easily corrupt the best natures and best-brought-up wits.

But I marvel the less that these misorders be amongst some in the court, for commonly in the country also everywhere innocency is gone, bashfulness is banished, much presumption in youth, small authority in age, reverence is neglected, duties be confounded, and, to be short, disobedience doth overflow the banks of good order, almost in every place, almost in every degree of man.

Mean men have eyes to see, and cause to lament, and occasion to complain of these miseries, but other have authority to remedy them, and will do so, too, when God shall think time fit. For all these misorders be God's just plagues, by his sufferance brought justly upon us for our sins, which be infinite in number and horrible in deed, but namely, for the great abominable sin of unkindness.[63] But what unkindness? Even such unkindness as was in the Jews in contemning God's voice, in shrinking from his word, in wishing back again for Egypt, in committing adultery and whoredom, not with the women, but with the doctrine, of Babylon, did bring all the plagues, destructions, and captivities that fell so oft and horribly upon Israel.

[62] The characters named are all slaves in comedies by Terence; a Geta also appears in the *Truculentus* of Plautus.
[63] Ingratitude.

## The Bringing-up of Youth

We have cause also in England to beware of unkindness, who have had in so few years the candle of God's word so oft lightened, so oft put out, and yet will venture by our unthankfulness in doctrine and sinful life to lose again light, candle, candlestick, and all.

God keep us in his fear; God graft in us the true knowledge of his word, with a forward will to follow it, and so to bring forth the sweet fruits of it, and then shall he preserve us by his grace from all manner of terrible days.

The remedy of this doth not stand only in making good common laws for the whole realm, but also (and perchance chiefly) in observing private discipline every man carefully in his own house, and namely, if special regard be had to youth, and that not so much in teaching them what is good as in keeping them from that that is ill.

Therefore, if wise fathers be not as well ware in weeding from their children ill things and ill company as they were before in grafting in them learning and providing for them good schoolmasters, what fruit they shall reap of all their cost and care common experience doth tell.

Here is the place, in youth is the time, when some ignorance is as necessary as much knowledge, and not in matters of our duty toward God, as some willful wits, willingly against their own knowledge, perniciously against their own conscience, have of late openly taught. Indeed St. Chrysostom, that noble and eloquent doctor, in a sermon *Contra fatum* and the curious searching of nativities, doth wisely say that ignorance therein is better than knowledge.[64] But to wring this sentence, to wrest thereby out of men's hands the knowledge of God's doctrine, is without all reason, against common sense, contrary to the judg-

[64] *Melius est enim bene ignorare, quam turpiter scire* (*De providentia Dei, ac fato orationes sex,* trans. John Cheke [London, 1545], Oratio quinta, sig. E3r).

45

ment also of them which be the discreetest men and best learned on their own side. I know Julianus Apostata did so,[65] but I never heard or read that any ancient father of the primitive church either thought or wrote so.

But this ignorance in youth which I spake on, or rather this simplicity, or most truly, this innocency, is that which the noble Persians, as wise Xenophon doth testify, were so careful to breed up their youth in. But Christian fathers commonly do not so. And I will tell you a tale as much to be misliked as the Persians' example is to be followed.

This last summer I was in a gentleman's house where a young child, somewhat past four year old, could in no wise frame his tongue to say a little short grace, and yet he could roundly rap out so many ugly oaths, and those of the newest fashion, as some good man of fourscore year old hath never heard named before; and that which was most detestable of all, his father and mother would laugh at it. I much doubt what comfort another day this child shall bring unto them. This child, using much the company of servingmen and giving good ear to their talk, did easily learn which he shall hardly forget all days of his life hereafter. So likewise in the court, if a young gentleman will venture himself into the company of ruffians, it is overgreat a jeopardy lest their fashions, manners, thoughts, talk, and deeds will very soon be ever like. The confounding of companies breedeth confusion of good manners both in the court and everywhere else.

And it may be a great wonder, but a greater shame, to us Christian men to understand what a heathen writer, Isocrates, doth leave in memory of writing concerning the care that the noble city of Athens had to bring up their youth in honest company and virtuous discipline; whose talk in Greek is to this effect in English:

[65] Julian forbade Christian professors to teach grammar and rhetoric (Ammianus Marcellinus, *The Histories*, XXII.x.7; XXV.iv.20).

## The Bringing-up of Youth

The city was not more careful to see their children well taught than to see their young men well governed, which they brought to pass not so much by common law as by private discipline. For they had more regard that their youth by good order should not offend than how by law they might be punished, and if offense were committed there was neither way to hide it, neither hope of pardon for it. Good natures were not so much openly praised as they were secretly marked and watchfully regarded, lest they should lose the goodness they had. Therefore in schools of singing and dancing, and other honest exercises, governors were appointed, more diligent to oversee their good manners than their masters were to teach them any learning. It was some shame to a young man to be seen in the open market, and if for business he passed through it, he did it with a marvelous modesty and bashful fashion. To eat or drink in a tavern was not only a shame but also punishable in a young man. To contrary or to stand in terms [66] with an old man was more heinous than in some place to rebuke and scold with his own father.[67]

With many other more good orders and fair disciplines, which I refer to their reading that have lust to look upon the description of such a worthy commonwealth.

And to know what worthy fruit did spring of such worthy seed, I will tell you the most marvel of all, and yet such a truth as no man shall deny it except such as be ignorant in knowledge of the best stories.[68]

Athens, by this discipline and good ordering of youth, did breed up within the circuit of that one city, within the compass of one hundred year, within the memory of one man's life, so many notable captains in war for worthiness, wisdom, and learning, as be scarce matchable, no, not in the state of Rome in the compass of those seven hundred years when it flourished most.

[66] Dispute.
[67] Ascham's "quotation" is a summary of details from *Areopagiticus,* paragraphs 37–49 *passim.*
[68] Histories.

47

And because I will not only say it but also prove it, the names of them be these: Miltiades, Themistocles, Xantippus, Pericles, Cymon, Alcibiades, Thrasybulus, Conon, Iphicrates, Xenophon, Timotheus, Theopompus, Demetrius, and divers other more; of which every one may justly be spoken that worthy praise which was given to Scipio Africanus, who Cicero doubteth whether he were more noble captain in war or more eloquent and wise counselor in peace. And if he believe not me, read diligently Aemilius Probus in Latin and Plutarch in Greek, which two had no cause either to flatter or lie upon any of those which I have recited.

And beside nobility in war, for excellent and matchless masters in all manner of learning, in that one city, in memory of one age, were more learned men, and that in a manner all together, than all time doth remember, than all place doth afford, than all other tongues do contain. And I do not mean of those authors which by injury of time, by negligence of men, by cruelty of fire and sword, be lost, but even of those which by God's grace are left yet unto us, of which, I thank God, even my poor study lacketh not one. As, in philosophy, Plato, Aristotle, Xenophon, Euclid, and Theophrastus; in eloquence and civil law, Demosthenes, Aeschines, Lycurgus, Dinarchus, Demades, Isocrates, Isaeus, Lysias, Antisthenes, Andocides; in histories, Herodotus, Thucydides, Xenophon, and which we lack, to our great loss, Theopompus and Ephorus; in poetry, Aeschylus, Sophocles, Euripides, Aristophanes, and somewhat of Menander, Demosthenes' sister's son.

Now let Italian, and Latin itself, Spanish, French, Dutch,[69] and English bring forth their learning and recite their authors; Cicero only expected, and one or two more in Latin, they be all patched clouts and rags in comparison of fair-woven broadcloths. And truly, if there be any good in them, it is either

---

[69] German.

learned, borrowed, or stolen from some one of those worthy wits of Athens.

The remembrance of such a commonwealth, using such discipline and order for youth, and thereby bringing forth to their praise, and leaving to us for our example, such captains for war, such counselors for peace and matchless masters for all kind of learning, is pleasant for me to recite and not irksome, I trust, for other to hear, except it be such as make neither count of virtue nor learning.

And whether there be any such or no I cannot well tell; yet I hear say some young gentlemen of ours count it their shame to be counted learned, and perchance they count it their shame to be counted honest also, for I hear say they meddle as little with the one as with the other. A marvelous case: that gentlemen should so be ashamed of good learning and never a whit ashamed of ill manners; such do lay [70] for them that the gentlemen of France do so, which is a lie, as God will have it. Langaeus and Bellaeus,[71] that be dead, and the noble Vidame of Chartres,[72] that is alive, and infinite more in France which I hear tell of, prove this to be most false. And though some in France which will needs be gentlemen whether men will or no, and have more gentleship in their hat than in their head, be at deadly feud with both learning and honesty, yet I believe, if that noble prince King Francis the First were alive, they should have neither place in his court nor pension in his wars if he had knowledge of them. This opinion is not French, but plain Turkish, from whence some French fetch more faults than this, which, I pray, God keep out of England and send also those of ours better minds which bend themselves against virtue and

---

[70] Allege.

[71] The brothers Guillaume du Bellay, Seigneur de Langey, a noted soldier and diplomat, and Cardinal Jean du Bellay.

[72] Jean de Ferrières, who enjoyed a pension from Queen Elizabeth and whom no doubt Ascham had often seen at court.

learning, to the contempt of God, dishonor of their country, to the hurt of many others, and at length to the greatest harm and utter destruction of themselves.

Some other, having better nature but less wit (for ill commonly have overmuch wit) do not utterly dispraise learning, but they say that, without learning, common experience, knowledge of all fashions, and haunting all companies shall work in youth both wisdom and ability to execute any weighty affair. Surely long experience doth profit much, but most, and almost only, to him (if we mean honest affairs) that is diligently before instructed with precepts of well-doing. For good precepts of learning be the eyes of the mind to look wisely before a man, which way to go right and which not.

Learning teacheth more in one year than experience in twenty, and learning teacheth safely, when experience maketh more miserable than wise. He hazardeth sore that waxeth wise by experience. An unhappy master he is that is made cunning by many shipwrecks; a miserable merchant, that is neither rich nor wise but after some bankrupts. It is costly wisdom that is bought by experience. We know by experience itself that it is a marvelous pain to find out but a short way by long wandering. And surely he that would prove wise by experience, he may be witty indeed, but even like a swift runner that runneth fast out of his way and upon the night, he knoweth not whither. And verily they be fewest of number that be happy or wise by unlearned experience. And look well upon the former life of those few, whether your example be old or young, who without learning have gathered by long experience a little wisdom and some happiness, and when you do consider what mischief they have committed, what dangers they have escaped (and yet twenty for one do perish in the adventure), then think well with yourself whether ye would that your own son should come to wisdom and happiness by the way of such experience or no.

It is a notable tale that old Sir Roger Cholmley, sometime

chief justice, would tell of himself. When he was ancient [73] in Inn of Court, certain young gentlemen were brought before him to be corrected for certain misorders, and one of the lustiest said, "Sir, we be young gentlemen, and wise men before us have proved [74] all fashions, and yet those have done full well." This they said because it was well known that Sir Roger had been a good fellow in his youth. But he answered them very wisely. "Indeed," saith he, "in youth I was as you are now, and I had twelve fellows like unto myself, but not one of them came to a good end. And therefore follow not my example in youth, but follow my counsel in age, if ever ye think to come to this place or to these years that I am come unto, lest ye meet either with poverty or Tyburn in the way."

Thus experience of all fashions in youth, being in proof always dangerous, in issue seldom lucky, is a way, indeed, to overmuch knowledge, yet used commonly of such men which be either carried by some curious affection of mind or driven by some hard necessity of life to hazard the trial of overmany perilous adventures.

Erasmus, the honor of learning of all our time, said wisely that experience is the common schoolhouse of fools and ill men; [75] men of wit and honesty be otherwise instructed. For there be that keep them out of fire and yet was never burned, that beware of water and yet was never nigh drowning, that hate harlots and was never at the stews, that abhor falsehood and never brake promise themselves.

But will ye see a fit similitude of this adventured experience? A father that doth let loose his son to all experiences is most like a fond hunter that letteth slip a whelp to the whole herd.

---

[73] A senior member of the governing body.       [74] Tried.

[75] *Experientia stultorum magistra* (*Opera omnia*, ed. J. Leclerc, I [Leyden, 1703], 901E); also illustrated at some length under *Factum stultus cognoscit* and *Malo accepto stultus sapit* in *Adagia* (*ibid.,* II [1706], 38E–39E).

Twenty to one, he shall fall upon a rascal [76] and let go the fair game. Men that hunt so be either ignorant persons, privy stealers, or nightwalkers.

Learning, therefore, ye wise fathers, and good bringing-up, and not blind and dangerous experience, is the next and readiest way that must lead your children, first to wisdom and then to worthiness, if ever ye purpose they shall come there.

And to say all in short, though I lack authority to give counsel, yet I lack not good will to wish that the youth in England, specially gentlemen, and namely nobility, should be by good bringing-up so grounded in judgment of learning, so founded in love of honesty as, when they should be called forth to the execution of great affairs in service of their prince and country, they might be able to use and to order all experiences, were they good, were they bad, and that according to the square, rule, and line of wisdom, learning, and virtue.

And I do not mean by all this my talk that young gentlemen should always be poring on a book, and by using good studies should lose honest pleasure and haunt no good pastime. I mean nothing less,[77] for it is well known that I both like and love, and have always and do yet still use, all exercises and pastimes that be fit for my nature and ability. And beside natural disposition, in judgment also I was never either Stoic in doctrine or Anabaptist in religion, to mislike a merry, pleasant, and playful nature, if no outrage be committed against law, measure, and good order.

Therefore I would wish that, beside some good time, fitly appointed and constantly kept, to increase by reading the knowledge of the tongues and learning, young gentlemen should use and delight in all courtly exercises and gentlemanlike pastimes. And good cause why: for the selfsame noble city of Athens, justly commended of me before, did wisely and upon

[76] A young deer without antlers, or a lean, inferior one.
[77] Anything but.

great consideration appoint the Muses, Apollo, and Pallas to be patrons of learning to their youth. For the Muses, besides learning, were also ladies of dancing, mirth, and minstrelsy; Apollo was god of shooting and author of cunning playing upon instruments; Pallas also was lady mistress in wars. Whereby was nothing else meant but that learning should be always mingled with honest mirth and comely exercises, and that war also should be governed by learning and moderated by wisdom, as did well appear in those captains of Athens named by me before, and also in Scipio and Caesar, the two diamonds of Rome.

And Pallas was no more feared in wearing *aegida* [78] than she was praised for choosing *oliva;* whereby shineth the glory of learning, which thus was governor and mistress in the noble city of Athens both of war and peace.

Therefore, to ride comely, to run fair at the tilt or ring, to play at all weapons, to shoot fair in bow or surely in gun, to vault [79] lustily, to run, to leap, to wrestle, to swim, to dance comely, to sing and play of instruments cunningly, to hawk, to hunt, to play at tennis, and all pastimes generally which be joined with labor, used in open place and on the daylight, containing either some fit exercise for war or some pleasant pastime for peace, be not only comely and decent but also very necessary for a courtly gentleman to use.

But of all kind of pastimes fit for a gentleman I will, God willing, in fitter place, more at large, declare fully in my book of the cockpit,[80] which I do write to satisfy some, I trust with some reason, that be more curious in marking other men's doings than careful in mending their own faults. And some also will needs busy themselves in marveling, and adding thereunto unfriendly

---

[78] The aegis.     [79] 1570: vant.

[80] No trace of such a work by Ascham has ever been found, but this allusion to it is linked with a tradition that he died poor because of an addiction to cockfighting and other forms of gambling.

talk, why I, a man of good years and of no ill place (I thank God and my prince), do make choice to spend such time in writing of trifles, as the school of shooting,[81] the cockpit, and this book of the first principles of grammar, rather than to take some weighty matter in hand either of religion or civil discipline.

Wise men, I know, will well allow of my choice herein, and as for such who have not wit of themselves but must learn of others to judge right of men's doings, let them read that wise poet Horace in his *Arte poetica*, who willeth wise men to beware of high and lofty titles. For great ships require costly tackling and also afterward dangerous[82] government; small boats be neither very chargeable in making nor very oft in great jeopardy, and yet they carry many times as good and costly ware as greater vessels do. A mean argument may easily bear the light burden of a small fault and have always at hand a ready excuse for ill handling, and some praise it is if it so chance to be better in deed than a man dare venture to seem. A high title doth charge a man with the heavy burden of too great a promise, and therefore saith Horace very wittily that that poet was a very fool that began his book with a goodly verse indeed but overproud a promise:

*Fortunam Priami cantabo et nobile bellum.*

And after, as wisely:

*Quanto rectius hic, qui nil molitur inepte, etc.,*[83]

meaning Homer, who, within the compass of a small argument of one harlot and one good wife, did utter so much learning in all kind of sciences as, by the judgment of Quintilian, he deserveth so high a praise that no man yet deserved to sit in the

[81] *Toxophilus.*     [82] Meticulous.

[83] *Ars poetica,* 137, 140: "I shall sing of the fate and famous war of Priam"; "How much more rightly he does who undertakes nothing impertinently."

# The Bringing-up of Youth

second degree beneath him.[84] And thus much out of my way, concerning my purpose in spending pen and paper and time upon trifles, and namely to answer some that have neither wit nor learning to do anything themselves, neither will nor honesty to say well of other.

To join learning with comely exercises, Conte Baldassare Castiglione in his book *Cortegiano* doth trimly teach; which book, advisedly read and diligently followed but one year at home in England, would do a young gentleman more good, iwis, than three years' travel abroad spent in Italy. And I marvel this book is no more read in the court than it is, seeing it is so well translated into English by a worthy gentleman, Sir Thomas Hoby, who was many ways well furnished with learning and very expert in knowledge of divers tongues.[85]

And beside good precepts in books in all kind of tongues, this court also never lacked many fair examples for young gentlemen to follow; and surely one example is more valuable, both to good and ill, then twenty precepts written in books, and so Plato, not in one or two but divers places, doth plainly teach.[86]

If King Edward had lived a little longer, his only example had bred such a race of worthy learned gentlemen as this realm never yet did afford.

And in the second degree, two noble primroses of nobility, the young Duke of Suffolk and Lord Henry Maltravers, were such two examples to the court for learning as our time may rather wish than look for again.

[84] *Institutio oratoria*, X.i.50–51.

[85] *Il Cortegiano*, most celebrated of Renaissance courtesy books, was published at Venice in 1528. Hoby's translation, *The Courtier*, appeared at London in 1561.

[86] For example, *Laws*, V.729C: "The most effective way of training the young—as well as the older people themselves—is not by admonition, but by plainly practising throughout one's own life the admonitions which one gives to others." Reprinted by permission of the publishers and the Loeb Classical Library from *Plato*, trans. R. G. Bury *et al.*, IX (Cambridge, Mass.: Harvard University Press, 1961), 331.

## The Schoolmaster

At Cambridge also, in St. John's College in my time, I do know that not so much the good statutes as two gentlemen of worthy memory, Sir John Cheke and Doctor Redman, by their only example of excellency in learning, of godliness in living, of diligency in studying, of counsel in exhorting, of good order in all thing, did breed up so many learned men in that one College of St. John's at one time as, I believe, the whole University of Louvain in many years was never able to afford.

Present examples of this present time I list not to touch; yet there is one example for all the gentlemen of this court to follow that may well satisfy them, or nothing will serve them, nor no example move them, to goodness and learning.

It is your shame (I speak to you all, you young gentlemen of England) that one maid should go beyond you all in excellency of learning and knowledge of divers tongues. Point forth six of the best-given gentlemen of this court, and all they together show not so much good will, spend not so much time, bestow not so many hours, daily, orderly, and constantly, for the increase of learning and knowledge as doth the Queen's Majesty herself. Yea, I believe that, beside her perfect readiness in Latin, Italian, French, and Spanish, she readeth here now at Windsor more Greek every day than some prebendary of this church doth read Latin in a whole week. And that which is most praiseworthy of all, within the walls of her privy chamber she hath obtained that excellency of learning, to understand, speak, and write, both wittily with head and fair with hand, as scarce one or two rare wits in both the universities have in many years reached unto. Amongst all the benefits that God hath blessed me withal, next the knowledge of Christ's true religion, I count this the greatest: that it pleased God to call me to be one poor minister in setting forward these excellent gifts of learning in this most excellent prince. Whose only example if the rest of our nobility would follow, then might England be, for learning and wisdom in nobility, a spectacle to all the world

*The Bringing-up of Youth*

beside. But see the mishap of men: the best examples have never such force to move to any goodness as the bad, vain, light, and fond have to all illness.

And one example, though out of the compass of learning, yet not out of the order of good manners, was notable in this court not fully twenty-four years ago, when all the acts of parliament, many good proclamations, divers strait commandments, sore punishment openly, special regard privately, could not do so much to take away one misorder as the example of one big one of this court did still to keep up the same. The memory whereof doth yet remain in a common proverb of Birchin Lane.[87]

Take heed, therefore, ye great ones in the court, yea, though ye be the greatest of all, take heed what ye do, take heed how ye live. For as you great ones use to do, so all mean men love to do. You be indeed makers or marrers of all men's manners within the realm. For though God hath placed you to be chief in making of laws, to bear greatest authority, to command all others, yet God doth order that all your laws, all your authority, all your commandments, do not half so much with mean men as doth your example and manner of living. And for example even in the greatest matter, if you yourselves do serve God gladly and orderly for conscience' sake, not coldly and sometime for manners' sake, you carry all the court with you, and the whole realm beside, earnestly and orderly to do the same. If you do otherwise, you be the only authors of all misorders in religion, not only to the court but to all England beside. Infinite shall be made cold in religion by your example that never were hurt by reading of books.

And in meaner matters, if three or four great ones in court will needs outrage in apparel—in huge hose, in monstrous hats, in garish colors—let the prince proclaim, make laws, order,

---

[87] A street in London. The allusion is obscure, though the expression "to send someone to Birchin Lane" is proverbial for having him whipped or flogged.

punish, command every gate in London daily to be watched, let all good men beside do everywhere what they can, surely the misorder of apparel in mean men abroad shall never be amended, except the greatest in court will order and mend themselves first. I know some great and good ones in court were authors that honest citizens of London should watch at every gate to take misordered persons in apparel. I know that honest Londoners did so, and I saw, which I saw then and report now with some grief, that some courtly men were offended with these good men of London. And that which grieved me most of all, I saw the very same time, for all these good orders commanded from the court and executed in London, I saw, I say, come out of London even unto the presence of the prince a great rabble of mean and light persons in apparel, for matter against law, for making against order, for fashion, namely hose, so without all order, as he thought himself most brave that durst do most in breaking order and was most monstrous in misorder. And for all the great commandments that came out of the court, yet this bold misorder was winked at and borne withal in the court. I thought it was not well that some great ones of the court durst declare themselves offended with good men of London for doing their duty, and the good ones of the court would not show themselves offended with ill men of London for breaking good order. I found thereby a saying of Socrates to be most true: that ill men be more hasty than good men be forward to prosecute their purposes, even as Christ himself saith of the children of light and darkness.[88]

Beside apparel, in all other things too, not so much good laws and strait commandments as the example and manner of living of great men doth carry all mean men everywhere to like and love and do as they do. For if but two or three noblemen in the court would but begin to shoot, all young gentlemen, the whole

[88] Plato, *Republic*, III.409C–D; Luke 16:8.

58

court, all London, the whole realm would straightway exercise shooting.

What praise should they win to themselves, what commodity should they bring to their country, that would thus deserve to be pointed at: "Behold, there goeth the author of good order, the guide of good men." I could say more, and yet not overmuch. But perchance some will say I have stepped too far out of my school into the commonwealth, from teaching a young scholar to monish great and noble men; yet I trust good and wise men will think and judge of me that my mind was not so much to be busy and bold with them that be great now as to give true advice to them that may be great hereafter. Who, if they do as I wish them to do, how great soever they be now by blood and other men's means, they shall become a great deal greater hereafter by learning, virtue, and their own deserts, which is true praise, right worthiness, and very nobility indeed. Yet if some will needs press me that I am too bold with great men and stray too far from my matter, I will answer them with St. Paul: *Sive per contentionem, sive quocumque modo, modo Christus praedicetur, etc.*[89] Even so, whether in place or out of place, with my matter or beside my matter, if I can hereby either provoke the good or stay the ill, I shall think my writing herein well employed.

But to come down from great men and higher matters to my little children and poor schoolhouse again, I will, God willing, go forward orderly as I purposed to instruct children and young men, both for learning and manners.

Hitherto I have showed what harm overmuch fear bringeth to children and what hurt ill company and overmuch liberty breedeth in youth, meaning thereby that from seven year old to seventeen love is the best allurement to learning, from seventeen to seven-and-twenty that wise men should carefully see the

[89] A rough summary of Phil. 1:15–18: "Whether out of contention, or in whatever manner, nevertheless Christ is preached."

steps of youth surely stayed by good order in that most slippery time, and specially in the court, a place most dangerous for youth to live in without great grace, good regard, and diligent looking to.

Sir Richard Sackville, that worthy gentleman of worthy memory, as I said in the beginning, in the Queen's privy chamber at Windsor, after he had talked with me for the right choice of a good wit in a child for learning, and of the true difference betwixt quick and hard wits, of alluring young children by gentleness to love learning, and of the special care that was to be had to keep young men from licentious living, he was most earnest with me to have me say my mind also what I thought concerning the fancy that many young gentlemen of England have to travel abroad, and namely to lead a long life in Italy. His request, both for his authority and good will toward me, was a sufficient commandment unto me to satisfy his pleasure with uttering plainly my opinion in that matter. "Sir," quoth I, "I take going thither and living there, for a young gentleman that doth not go under the keep and guard of such a man as both by wisdom can and authority dare rule him, to be marvelous dangerous." And why I said so then I will declare at large now; which I said then privately and write now openly, not because I do contemn either the knowledge of strange and divers tongues, and namely the Italian tongue, which next the Greek and Latin tongue I like and love above all other, or else because I do despise the learning that is gotten or the experience that is gathered in strange countries, or for any private malice that I bear to Italy, which country and, in it, namely Rome, I have always specially honored because time was when Italy and Rome have been, to the great good of us that now live, the best breeders and bringers-up of the worthiest men, not only for wise speaking, but also for well-doing, in all civil affairs, that ever was in the world. But now that time is gone and, though the place remain, yet the old and present manners do differ as far as black and white, as virtue and vice. Virtue once made that country mistress over all the world. Vice now maketh that country slave to them that before were glad to serve it. All men seeth it; they themselves confess it, namely, such as be best and wisest amongst them. For sin, by lust and vanity, hath and doth breed up everywhere common contempt of God's word, private contention in many families, open factions in every city, and so, making themselves bond to vanity and vice at home, they are content to bear the yoke of serving strangers abroad. Italy now is not that Italy that it was wont to be and therefore now not so fit a place as some do count it for young men to fetch either wisdom or honesty from thence. For surely they will make other but bad scholars that be so ill masters to themselves. Yet if a gentleman will needs travel into Italy, he shall do well to look on the life of the wisest traveler that ever traveled thither, set out by the wisest writer that ever spake with tongue (God's doctrine only excepted), and that is Ulysses in Homer. Ulysses and his travel, I wish our travelers to look upon, not so much to fear them with the great dangers that he many times suffered as to instruct them with his excellent wisdom, which he always and everywhere used. Yea, even those that be learned and witty travelers, when they be disposed to praise traveling, as a great commendation and the best scripture they have for it, they gladly recite the third verse of Homer in his first book of *Odyssea*, containing a great praise of Ulysses for the wit he gathered and wisdom he used in his traveling.

Which verse—because in mine opinion it was not made at the first more naturally in Greek by Homer, nor after turned more aptly into Latin by Horace, than it was a good while ago in Cambridge translated into English, both plainly for the sense and roundly for the verse, by one of the best scholars that ever St. John's College bred, Master Watson, mine old friend, sometime Bishop of Lincoln—therefore, for their sake that have lust to see how our English tongue, in avoiding barbarous rhyming,

## The Schoolmaster

may as well receive right quantity of syllables and true order of versifying [90] (of which matter more at large hereafter) as either Greek or Latin, if a cunning man have it in handling, I will set forth that one verse in all three tongues for an example to good wits that shall delight in like learned exercise:

### Homerus

Πολλῶν δ'ἀνθρώπων ἴδεν ἄστεα καὶ νόον ἔγνω.

### Horatius

*Qui mores hominum multorum vidit et urbes.*

### Master Watson

All travelers do gladly report great praise of Ulysses,
For that he knew many men's manners, and saw many cities.

And yet is not Ulysses commended so much nor so oft in Homer because he was πολύτροπος, that is, skillful in many men's manners and fashions, as because he was πολύμητις, that is, wise in all purposes and ware in all places; which wisdom and wariness will not serve neither a traveler except Pallas be always at his elbow, that is, God's special grace from heaven, to keep him in God's fear in all his doings, in all his journey. For he shall not always, in his absence out of England, light upon a gentle Alcinous and walk in his fair gardens full of all harmless pleasures, but he shall sometimes fall either into the hands of some cruel Cyclops or into the lap of some wanton and dallying Dame Calypso, and so suffer the danger of many a deadly den, not so full of perils to destroy the body as full of vain pleasures to poison the mind. Some Siren shall sing him a song, sweet in tune, but sounding in the end to his utter destruction. If Scylla drown him not, Charybdis may fortune [91] swallow him. Some Circe shall make him, of a plain Englishman, a right Italian. And at length to hell, or to some hellish place, is he likely to go, from whence is hard returning, although one Ulysses, and that

[90] 1570: verifying.  [91] Happen to.

62

by Pallas' aid and good counsel of Teiresias, once escaped that horrible den of deadly darkness.

Therefore, if wise men will needs send their sons into Italy, let them do it wisely, under the keep and guard of him who, by his wisdom and honesty, by his example and authority, may be able to keep them safe and sound in the fear of God, in Christ's true religion, in good order and honesty of living, except they will have them run headlong into overmany jeopardies, as Ulysses had done many times if Pallas had not always governed him, if he had not used to stop his ears with wax, to bind himself to the mast of his ship, to feed daily upon that sweet herb *moly* with the black root and white flower, given unto him by Mercury to avoid all the enchantments of Circe.[92] Whereby the divine poet Homer meant covertly (as wise and godly men do judge) that love of honesty and hatred of ill which David more plainly doth call the fear of God, the only remedy against all enchantments of sin.[93]

I know divers noble personages and many worthy gentlemen of England whom all the Siren songs of Italy could never untwine from the mast of God's word, nor no enchantment of vanity overturn them from the fear of God and love of honesty.

But I know as many, or more, and some sometime my dear friends, for whose sake I hate going into that country the more, who, parting out of England fervent in the love of Christ's doctrine and well furnished with the fear of God, returned out of Italy worse transformed than ever was any in Circe's court. I know divers that went out of England men of innocent life, men of excellent learning, who returned out of Italy not only with worse manners but also with less learning, neither so willing to live orderly nor yet so able to speak learnedly as they were at home before they went abroad. And why? Plato, that wise writer and worthy traveler himself, telleth the cause why. He went into Sicilia, a country no nigher Italy by site of place than

[92] *Odyssey*, X.302–306.       [93] Psalms 33:16–19; compare 34:9–15.

Italy that is now is like Sicilia that was then in all corrupt manners and licentiousness of life. Plato found in Sicilia every city full of vanity, full of factions, even as Italy is now. And as Homer, like a learned poet, doth feign that Circe by pleasant enchantments did turn men into beasts, some into swine, some into asses, some into foxes, some into wolves, etc., even so Plato, like a wise philosopher, doth plainly declare that pleasure, by licentious vanity, that sweet and perilous poison of all youth, doth engender in all those that yield up themselves to her four notorious properties:

1. λήθην
2. δυσμαθίαν
3. ἀφροσύνην
4. ὕβριν.[94]

The first, forgetfulness of all good things learned before; the second, dullness to receive either learning or honesty ever after; the third, a mind embracing lightly the worse opinion and barren of discretion to make true difference betwixt good and ill, betwixt truth and vanity; the fourth, a proud disdainfulness of other good men in all honest matters. Homer and Plato have both one meaning, look both to one end. For if a man englut himself with vanity or welter in filthiness like a swine, all learning, all goodness, is soon forgotten. Then quickly shall he become a dull ass to understand either learning or honesty, and yet shall he be as subtle as a fox in breeding of mischief, in bringing in misorder, with a busy head, a discoursing tongue, and a factious heart, in every private affair, in all matters of state, with this pretty property: always glad to commend the worse party and ever ready to defend the falser opinion. And why? For, where will is given from goodness to vanity, the mind is soon carried from right judgment to any fond opinion in religion, in philosophy, or any other kind of

[94] Plato, *Epistles to Dionysius*, III.315C. The Greek terms mean forgetfulness, intellectual laziness, witlessness, and insolence.

*64*

learning. The fourth fruit of vain pleasure, by Homer and Plato's judgment, is pride in themselves, contempt of others, the very badge of all those that serve in Circe's court. The true meaning of both Homer and Plato is plainly declared in one short sentence of the holy prophet of God Jeremiah, crying out of the vain and vicious life of the Israelites. "This people," saith he, "be fools and dullheads to all goodness, but subtle, cunning, and bold in any mischief," etc.[95]

The true medicine against the enchantments of Circe, the vanity of licentious pleasure, the enticements of all sin, is, in Homer, the herb *moly*, with the black root and white flower, sour at the first but sweet in the end, which Hesiodus termeth the study of virtue, hard and irksome in the beginning but in the end easy and pleasant.[96] And that which is most to be marveled at, the divine poet Homer saith plainly that this medicine against sin and vanity is not found out by man but given and taught by God. And for someone's sake that will have delight to read that sweet and godly verse, I will recite the very words of Homer and also turn them into rude English meter:

Χαλεπὸν δέ τ' ὀρύσσειν
ἀνδράσι γε θνητοῖσι, θεοὶ δέ τε πάντα δύνανται.[97]

In English thus:

> No mortal man, with sweat of brow, or toil of mind,
> But only God, who can do all, that herb doth find.

Plato also, that divine philosopher, hath many godly medicines against the poison of vain pleasure in many places, but

[95] Jer. 4:22.

[96] Hesiod, *Works and Days*, 289–292: "But between us and Goodness the gods have placed the sweat of our brows: long and steep is the path that leads to her, and it is rough at the first; but when a man has reached the top, then indeed she is easy, though otherwise hard to reach." Reprinted by permission of the publishers and the Loeb Classical Library from Hesiod, *The Homeric Hymns and Homerica*, trans. Hugh C. Evelyn-White (Cambridge, Mass.: Harvard University Press, 1964), p. 25.

[97] *Odyssey*, X.305–306.

especially in his epistles to Dionysius the tyrant of Sicily; yet against those that will needs become beasts with serving of Circe the prophet David crieth most loud: *Nolite fieri sicut equus et mulus,* and by and by giveth the right medicine, the true herb *moly: In camo et freno maxillas eorum constringe;*[98] that is to say, "Let God's grace be the bit, let God's fear be the bridle to stay them from running headlong into vice and to turn them into the right way again." David in the second psalm after giveth the same medicine, but in these plainer words: *Diverte a malo, et fac bonum.*[99] But I am afraid that overmany of our travelers into Italy do not eschew the way to Circe's court but go and ride and run and fly thither; they make great haste to come to her; they make great suit to serve her; yea, I could point out some with my finger that never had gone out of England but only to serve Circe in Italy. Vanity and vice and any license to ill-living in England was counted stale and rude unto them. And so, being mules and horses before they went, returned very swine and asses home again; yet everywhere very foxes with subtle and busy heads and, where they may, very wolves with cruel malicious hearts. A marvelous monster which for filthiness of living, for dullness to learning himself, for wiliness in dealing with others, for malice in hurting without cause, should carry at once in one body the belly of a swine, the head of an ass, the brain of a fox, the womb of a wolf. If you think we judge amiss and write too sore against you, hear what the Italian saith of the Englishman, what the master reporteth of the scholar, who uttereth plainly what is taught by him and what is learned by you, saying, *Inglese italianato è un diavolo incarnato;* that is to say, "You remain men in shape and fashion but become devils in life and condition." This is not the opinion

[98] Psalms 32:9 (Vulgate 31:9): "Be not as the horse, or as the mule, which have no understanding: whose mouth must be held in with bit and bridle, lest they come near unto thee."

[99] Psalms 34:14 (Vulgate 33:15): "Depart from evil, and do good."

of one for some private spite but the judgment of all in a common proverb which riseth of that learning and those manners which you gather in Italy, a good schoolhouse of wholesome doctrine, and worthy masters of commendable scholars, where the master had rather defame himself for his teaching than not shame his scholar for his learning. A good nature of the master and fair conditions of the scholars. And now choose you, you Italian Englishmen, whether you will be angry with us for calling you monsters, or with the Italians for calling you devils, or else with your own selves, that take so much pains and go so far to make yourselves both. If some yet do not well understand what is an Englishman Italianated, I will plainly tell him: he that by living and traveling in Italy bringeth home into England out of Italy the religion, the learning, the policy, the experience, the manners of Italy. That is to say, for religion, papistry or worse; for learning, less, commonly, than they carried out with them; for policy, a factious heart, a discoursing head, a mind to meddle in all men's matters; for experience, plenty of new mischiefs never known in England before; for manners, variety of vanities and change of filthy living. These be the enchantments of Circe brought out of Italy to mar men's manners in England: much by example of ill life but more by precepts of fond books, of late translated out of Italian into English, sold in every shop in London, commended by honest titles the sooner to corrupt honest manners, dedicated overboldly to virtuous and honorable personages, the easilier to beguile simple and innocent wits. It is pity that those which have authority and charge to allow and disallow books to be printed be no more circumspect herein than they are. Ten sermons at Paul's Cross [100] do not so much good for moving men to true doctrine as one of those books do harm with enticing men to ill-living.

[100] A famous pulpit surmounted with a cross that formerly stood outside St. Paul's Cathedral, London, where many famous sermons were preached in Tudor and Stuart times.

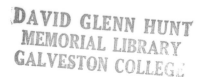

Yea, I say farther, those books tend not so much to corrupt honest living as they do to subvert true religion. More papists be made by your merry books of Italy than by your earnest books of Louvain. And because our great physicians do wink at the matter and make no count of this sore, I, though not admitted one of their fellowship, yet having been many years a prentice to God's true religion, and trust to continue a poor journeyman therein all days of my life, for the duty I owe and love I bear both to true doctrine and honest living, though I have no authority to amend the sore myself, yet I will declare my good will to discover the sore to others.

St. Paul saith that sects and ill opinions be the works of the flesh and fruits of sin.[101] This is spoken no more truly for the doctrine than sensibly for the reason. And why? For ill-doings breed ill-thinkings, and of corrupted manners spring perverted judgments. And how? There be in man two special things: man's will, man's mind. Where will inclineth to goodness the mind is bent to truth; where will is carried from goodness to vanity the mind is soon drawn from truth to false opinion. And so the readiest way to entangle the mind with false doctrine is first to entice the will to wanton living. Therefore, when the busy and open papists abroad could not by their contentious books turn men in England fast enough from truth and right judgment in doctrine, then the subtle and secret papists at home procured bawdy books to be translated out of the Italian tongue, whereby overmany young wills and wits, allured to wantonness, do now boldly contemn all severe books that sound to honesty and godliness. In our forefathers' time, when papistry as a standing pool covered and overflowed all England, few books were read in our tongue, saving certain books of chivalry, as they said, for pastime and pleasure, which, as some say, were made in monasteries by idle monks or wanton canons; as one for example, *Morte Darthur,* the whole pleasure of which book

[101] Gal. 5:20.

standeth in two special points—in open manslaughter and bold bawdry; in which book those be counted the noblest knights that do kill most men without any quarrel and commit foulest adulteries by subtlest shifts: as Sir Lancelot with the wife of King Arthur his master, Sir Tristram with the wife of King Mark his uncle, Sir Lamorak with the wife of King Lot that was his own aunt. This is good stuff for wise men to laugh at or honest men to take pleasure at. Yet I know when God's Bible was banished the court and *Morte Darthur* received into the prince's chamber. What toys [102] the daily reading of such a book may work in the will of a young gentleman or a young maid that liveth wealthily and idly, wise men can judge and honest men do pity. And yet ten *Morte Darthurs* do not the tenth part so much harm as one of these books made in Italy and translated in England. They open, not fond and common ways to vice, but such subtle, cunning, new, and diverse shifts to carry young wills to vanity and young wits to mischief, to teach old bawds new school points, as the simple head of an Englishman is not able to invent, nor never was heard of in England before, yea, when papistry overflowed all. Suffer these books to be read, and they shall soon displace all books of godly learning. For they, carrying the will to vanity and marring good manners, shall easily corrupt the mind with ill opinions and false judgment in doctrine, first to think ill of all true religion, and at last to think nothing of God himself, one special point that is to be learned in Italy and Italian books. And that which is most to be lamented, and therefore more needful to be looked to, there be more of these ungracious books set out in print within these few months than have been seen in England many score years before. And because our Englishmen made Italians cannot hurt but certain persons and in certain places, therefore these Italian books are made English to bring mischief enough openly and boldly to all states, great and mean, young and old, everywhere.

[102] Fantastic or wanton notions.

And thus you see how will enticed to wantonness doth easily allure the mind to false opinions and how corrupt manners in living breed false judgment in doctrine, how sin and fleshliness bring forth sects and heresies; and therefore suffer not vain books to breed vanity in men's wills if you would have God's truth take root in men's minds.

That Italian that first invented the Italian proverb against our Englishmen Italianated meant no more their vanity in living than their lewd opinion in religion, for in calling them devils he carrieth them clean from God; and yet he carrieth them no farther than they willingly go themselves, that is, where they may freely say their minds to the open contempt of God and all godliness both in living and doctrine.

And how? I will express how, not by a fable of Homer nor by the philosophy of Plato, but by a plain truth of God's word, sensibly uttered by David thus: these men, *abominabiles facti in studiis suis*, think verily and sing gladly the verse before: *Dixit insipiens in corde suo, non est Deus;* [103] that is to say, they, giving themselves up to vanity, shaking off the motions of grace, driving from them the fear of God, and running headlong into all sin, first lustily contemn God, then scornfully mock his word, and also spitefully hate and hurt all well-willers thereof. Then they have in more reverence the *Triumphs* of Petrarch than the Genesis of Moses; they make more account of Tully's *Offices* than St. Paul's Epistles, of a tale in Boccaccio than a story of the Bible. Then they count as fables the holy mysteries of Christian religion. They make Christ and his gospel only serve civil policy; then neither religion cometh amiss to them; in time they be promoters of both openly, in place again mockers of both privily, as I wrote once in a rude rhyme:

Now new, now old, now both, now neither,
To serve the world's course, they care not with whether.

---

[103] Psalms 14:1–2 (Vulgate 13:1–2): "The fool hath said in his heart, There is no God. They are corrupt, they have done abominable works, there is none that doeth good."

## The Bringing-up of Youth

For where they dare, in company where they like, they boldly laugh to scorn both Protestant and papist. They care for no Scripture; they make no count of general councils; they contemn the consent of the church; they pass for no doctors; they mock the Pope; they rail on Luther; they allow neither side; they like none but only themselves; the mark they shoot at, the end they look for, the heaven they desire, is only their own present pleasure and private profit; whereby they plainly declare of whose school, of what religion, they be; that is, epicures in living and ἄθεοι [104] in doctrine. This last word is no more unknown now to plain Englishmen than the person was unknown sometime in England, until some Englishman took pains to fetch that devilish opinion out of Italy. These men, thus Italianated abroad, cannot abide our godly Italian church at home: they be not of that parish; they be not of that fellowship; they like not the preacher; they hear not his sermons; except sometimes for company they come thither to hear the Italian tongue naturally spoken, not to hear God's doctrine truly preached.

And yet these men, in matters of divinity, openly pretend a great knowledge, and have privately to themselves a very compendious understanding of all, which nevertheless they will utter when and where they list. And that is this: all the mysteries of Moses, the whole law and ceremonies, the psalms and prophets, Christ and his gospel, GOD and the devil, heaven and hell, faith, conscience, sin, death, and all they shortly wrap up, they quickly expound with this one half-verse of Horace: *Credat Judaeus Apella*.[105]

Yet though in Italy they may freely be of no religion (as they are in England in very deed, too), nevertheless, returning home into England, they must countenance the profession of the one

[104] Atheists.
[105] *Satires*, I.v.100: "Let Apella the Jew believe it." The pagan Romans regarded the Jews as exceptionally superstitious in their religious doctrine and practices.

or the other, howsoever inwardly they laugh to scorn both. And though for their private matters they can follow, fawn, and flatter noble personages contrary to them in all respects, yet commonly they ally themselves with the worst papists, to whom they be wedded and do well agree together in three proper opinions: in open contempt of God's word, in a secret security of sin, and in a bloody desire to have all taken away, by sword or burning, that be not of their faction. They that do read with indifferent judgment Pighius [106] and Machiavelli, two indifferent patriarchs of these two religions, do know full well that I say true.

Ye see what manners and doctrine our Englishmen fetch out of Italy, for, finding no other there, they can bring no other hither. And therefore many godly and excellent learned Englishmen, not many years ago, did make a better choice, when open cruelty drave them out of this country, to place themselves there where Christ's doctrine, the fear of God, punishment of sin, and discipline of honesty were had in special regard.[107]

I was once in Italy myself, but, I thank God, my abode there was but nine days. And yet I saw in that little time, in one city, more liberty to sin than ever I heard tell of in our noble city of London in nine year. I saw it was there as free to sin, not only without all punishment but also without any man's marking, as it is free in the city of London to choose, without all blame, whether a man lust to wear shoe or pantofle.[108] And good cause why: for being unlike in truth of religion, they must needs be unlike in honesty of living. For, blessed be Christ, in our city of London commonly the commandments of God be more diligently taught and the service of God more reverently used, and that daily in many private men's houses, than they be in Italy

[106] Albert Pighius, or Pigghe (ca. 1490–1542), Dutch theologian and apologist for Catholicism against the German Protestant reformers.
[107] That is, in Protestant centers such as Zürich and Strasbourg.
[108] Slipper. 1570: pantocle.

once a week in their common churches, where masking ceremonies to delight the eye and vain sounds to please the ear do
quite thrust out of the churches all service of God in spirit and
truth. Yea, the Lord Mayor of London, being but a civil officer,
is commonly for his time more diligent in punishing sin, the
bent enemy against God and good order, than all the bloody
inquisitors in Italy be in seven year. For their care and charge
is not to punish sin, not to amend manners, not to purge
doctrine, but only to watch and oversee that Christ's true religion set no sure footing where the Pope hath any jurisdiction. I
learned when I was at Venice that there it is counted good
policy, when there be four or five brethren of one family, one
only to marry and all the rest to welter with as little shame in
open lechery as swine do here in the common mire. Yea, there
be as fair houses of religion, as great provision, as diligent
officers, to keep up this misorder, as Bridewell is, and all the
masters there, to keep down misorder. And therefore if the Pope
himself do not only grant pardons to further these wicked
purposes abroad in Italy, but also (although this present
Pope [109] in the beginning made some show of misliking thereof)
assign both meed and merit to the maintenance of stews and
brothel houses at home in Rome, then let wise men think Italy a
safe place for wholesome doctrine and godly manners and a fit
school for young gentlemen of England to be brought up in.

Our Italians bring home with them other faults from Italy,
though not so great as this of religion, yet a great deal greater
than many good men can well bear. For commonly they come
home common contemners of marriage and ready persuaders of
all other to the same, not because they love virginity nor yet
because they hate pretty young virgins, but being free in Italy
to go whithersoever lust will carry them, they do not like that

[109] Ascham clearly means St. Pius V, Pope from 1566 to 1572, since in
the earlier manuscript version of *The Schoolmaster* (fol. 75v), finished
before Pius' election, this parenthetical statement does not occur.

73

law and honesty should be such a bar to their like liberty at home in England. And yet they be the greatest makers of love, the daily dalliers, with such pleasant words, with such smiling and secret countenances, with such signs, tokens, wagers purposed to be lost before they were purposed to be made, with bargains of wearing colors, flowers, and herbs to breed occasion of ofter meeting of him and her and bolder talking of this and that, etc. And although I have seen some, innocent of all ill and staid in all honesty, that have used these things without all harm, without all suspicion of harm, yet these knacks [110] were brought first into England by them that learned them before in Italy in Circe's court, and how courtly courtesies soever they be counted now, yet if the meaning and manners of some that do use them were somewhat amended, it were no great hurt neither to themselves nor to others.

Another property of these [111] our English Italians is to be marvelous singular in all their matters: singular in knowledge, ignorant of nothing; so singular in wisdom (in their own opinion) as scarce they count the best counselor the prince hath comparable with them; common discoursers of all matters; busy searchers of most secret affairs; open flatterers of great men; privy mislikers of good men; fair speakers, with smiling countenances and much courtesy, openly to all men; ready backbiters, sore nippers, and spiteful reporters privily of good men. And being brought up in Italy, in some free city, as all cities be there, where a man may freely discourse against what he will, against whom he lust—against any prince, against any government, yea, against God himself and his whole religion—where he must be either Guelf or Ghibelline, either French or Spanish, and, always compelled to be of some party, of some faction, he shall never be compelled to be of any religion, and if he meddle not overmuch with Christ's true religion, he shall have free liberty to embrace all religions and become, if he lust, at once,

[110] Crafty devices.　　[111] 1570: this.

without any let or punishment, Jewish, Turkish, papish, and devilish.

A young gentleman thus bred up in this goodly school to learn the next and ready way to sin, to have a busy head, a factious heart, a talkative tongue, fed with discoursing of factions, led to contemn God and his religion, shall come home into England but very ill taught, either to be an honest man himself, a quiet subject to his prince, or willing to serve God under the obedience of true doctrine or within the order of honest living.

I know none will be offended with this my general writing but only such as find themselves guilty privately therein, who shall have good leave to be offended with me until they begin to amend themselves. I touch not them that be good, and I say too little of them that be nought. And so, though not enough for their deserving, yet sufficiently for this time, and more else when if occasion so require.

And thus far have I wandered from my first purpose of teaching a child, yet not altogether out of the way, because this whole talk hath tended to the only advancement of truth in religion and [112] honesty of living, and hath been wholly within the compass of learning and good manners, the special points belonging in the right bringing-up of youth.

But to my matter. As I began plainly and simply with my young scholar, so will I not leave him, God willing, until I have brought him a perfect scholar out of the school and placed him in the university to become a fit student for logic and rhetoric, and so after to physic,[113] law, or divinity, as aptness of nature, advice of friends, and God's disposition shall lead him.

[112] 1570: an.    [113] Medicine.

## THE END OF THE FIRST BOOK

# *The second book*

AFTER that your scholar, as I said before, shall come indeed, first, to a ready perfectness in translating, then, to a ripe and skillful choice in marking out his six points, as:

1. *Proprium*
2. *Translatum*
3. *Synonymum*
4. *Contrarium*
5. *Diversum*
6. *Phrases,*

then take this order with him: read daily unto him some book of Tully, as the third book of *Epistles* chosen out by Sturmius, *De amicitia, De senectute,* or that excellent epistle containing almost the whole first book *Ad Quintum fratrem;* [1] some comedy of Terence or Plautus (but in Plautus skillful choice must be used by the master to train his scholar to a judgment in cutting out perfectly overold and unproper words); Caesar's

---

[1] Epistle I.i, of Cicero's *Letters to His Brother Quintus,* no doubt recommended by Ascham for young gentlemen to translate because it contains excellent advice to Quintus on how to govern the province of Asia during his term as propraetor.

*Commentaries* are to be read with all curiosity, [where]in [2] specially without all exception to be made, either by friend or foe, is seen the unspotted propriety of the Latin tongue even when it was, as the Grecians say, in ακμῇ, that is, at the highest pitch of all perfectness; or some orations of Titus Livius, such as be both longest and plainest.

These books I would have him read now a good deal at every lecture, for he shall not now use daily translation but only construe again and parse where ye suspect is any need; yet let him not omit in these books his former exercise in marking diligently and writing orderly out his six points. And for translating, use you yourself, every second or third day, to choose out some epistle *Ad Atticum*, some notable commonplace out of his orations, or some other part of Tully, by your discretion, which your scholar may not know where to find, and translate it you yourself into plain, natural English, and then give it him to translate into Latin again, allowing him good space and time to do it both with diligent heed and good advisement. Here his wit shall be new set on work, his judgment for right choice truly tried, his memory for sure retaining better exercised than by learning anything without the book, and here how much he hath profited shall plainly appear. When he bringeth it translated unto you, bring you forth the place of Tully. Lay them together; compare the one with the other; commend his good choice and right placing of words. Show his faults gently, but blame them not oversharply; for of such missings, gently admonished of, proceedeth glad and good heed-taking; of good heed-taking springeth chiefly knowledge, which after groweth to perfectness if this order be diligently used by the scholar and gently handled by the master; for here shall all the hard points of grammar both easily and surely be learned up, which scholars in common schools, by making of Latins, be groping at with

[2] 1570: in.

## The Ready Way to the Latin Tongue

care and fear, and yet in many years they scarce can reach unto them. I remember when I was young, in the North, they went to the grammar school little children; they came from thence great lubbers,[3] always learning and little profiting: learning without book everything, understanding within the book little or nothing. Their whole knowledge, by learning without the book, was tied only to their tongue and lips, and never ascended up to the brain and head, and therefore was soon spit out of the mouth again. They were as men always going, but ever out of the way. And why? For their whole labor, or rather great toil without order, was even vain idleness without profit. Indeed, they took great pains about learning but employed small labor in learning, when by this way prescribed in this book, being straight, plain, and easy, the scholar is always laboring with pleasure and ever going right on forward with profit. Always laboring, I say, for or [4] he have construed, parsed, twice translated over by good advisement, marked out his six points by skillful judgment, he shall have necessary occasion to read over every lecture a dozen times, at the least. Which, because he shall do always in order, he shall do it always with pleasure. And pleasure allureth love; love hath lust to labor; labor always obtaineth his purpose, as most truly both Aristotle in his *Rhetoric* and *Oedipus* in Sophocles do teach saying: Πᾶν γὰρ ἐκπονούμενον ἅλισκε, *etc.*[5] And this oft reading is the very right following of that good counsel which Pliny doth give to his friend Fuscus, saying, *multum, non multa.*[6] But to my purpose again.

When, by this diligent and speedy reading over those forenamed good books of Tully, Terence, Caesar, and Livy, and by

[3] Stupid fellows.     [4] Before.

[5] Sophocles' words, assigned to Creon, are actually Τὸ δὲ ζητούμενον ἁλωτόν: "Who seeks shall find" (*Oedipus Rex*, 109–110). See also p. 30, n. 36.

[6] *Letters*, VII.ix.6: "Though we should read much, we should not read many books."

this second kind of translating out of your English, time shall breed skill, and use shall bring perfection, then ye may try, if you will, your scholar with the third kind of translation, although the two first ways, by mine opinion, be not only sufficient of themselves but also surer, both for the master's teaching and scholar's learning, than this third way is. Which is thus: write you in English some letter, as it were from him to his father or to some other friend, naturally, according to the disposition of the child, or some tale, or fable, or plain narration, according as Aphthonius beginneth his exercises of learning,[7] and let him translate it into Latin again, abiding in such place where no other scholar may prompt him. But yet use you yourself such discretion for choice therein as the matter may be within the compass, both for words and sentences, of his former learning and reading. And now take heed lest your scholar do not better in some point than you yourself, except ye have been diligently exercised in these kinds of translating before.

I had once a proof hereof, tried by good experience by a dear friend of mine when I came first from Cambridge to serve the Queen's Majesty, then Lady Elizabeth, lying at worthy Sir Anthony Denny's in Cheshunt. John Whitney, a young gentleman, was my bedfellow, who, willing by good nature and provoked by mine advice, began to learn the Latin tongue after the order declared in this book. We began after Christmas; I read unto him Tully *De amicitia,* which he did every day twice translate, out of Latin into English and out of English into Latin again. About St. Laurence' tide[8] after, to prove how he profited, I did choose out Torquatus' talk *de amicitia* in the latter end of the first book *De finibus*[9] because that place was

---

[7] "Fable" and "Narration" are the first two exercises in composition in the *Progymnasmata* of the Greek rhetorician Aphthonius, a work used widely in grammar schools during the Renaissance.

[8] August 10.      [9] Cicero, *De finibus bonorum et malorum,* I.xx.65–66.

the same in matter, like in words and phrases, nigh to the form and fashion of sentences, as he had learned before in *De amicitia*. I did translate it myself into plain English and gave it him to turn into Latin, which he did so choicely, so orderly, so without any great miss in the hardest points of grammar, that some in seven year in grammar schools, yea, and some in the universities too, cannot do half so well. This worthy young gentleman, to my greatest grief, to the great lamentation of that whole house, and specially to that most noble lady, now Queen Elizabeth herself, departed within few days out of this world.

And if in any cause a man may without offense of God speak somewhat ungodly, surely it was some grief unto me to see him hie so hastily to God as he did. A court full of such young gentlemen were rather a paradise than a court upon earth. And though I had never poetical head to make any verse in any tongue, yet either love, or sorrow, or both, did wring out of me then certain careful thoughts of my good will toward him which, in my mourning for him, fell forth more by chance than either by skill or use into this kind of misorderly meter:

Mine own John Whitney, now farewell, now death doth
    part us twain;
No death, but parting for a while, whom life shall join
    again.
Therefore, my heart, cease sighs and sobs, cease sorrow's
    seed to sow,
Whereof no gain, but greater grief, and hurtful care may
    grow.
Yet when I think upon such gifts of grace as God him
    lent,
My loss, his gain, I must a while with joyful tears lament.
Young years to yield such fruit in court, where seed of
    vice is sown,
Is sometime read, in some place seen, amongst us seldom
    known.

His life he led Christ's lore to learn, with will [10] to
work the same;
He read to know, and knew to live, and lived to praise his
name.
So fast to friend, so foe to few, so good to every wight,
I may well wish, but scarcely hope, again to have in sight.
The greater joy his life to me, his death the greater
pain;
His life in Christ so surely set doth glad my heart again.
His life so good, his death better, do mingle mirth with
care,
My spirit with joy, my flesh with grief, so dear a friend to
spare.
Thus God the good, while they be good, doth take,
and leave us ill,
That we should mend our sinful life, in life to tarry still.
Thus we well left, he [11] better reft,[12] in heaven to take
his place,
That by like life and death at last we may obtain like grace.
Mine own John Whitney, again farewell, a while
thus part in twain:
Whom pain doth part in earth, in heaven great joy shall
join again.

In this place, or I proceed farther, I will now declare by
whose authority I am led and by what reason I am moved to
think that this way of double translation out of one tongue into
another is [13] either only, or at least chiefly, to be exercised,
specially of youth, for the ready and sure obtaining of any
tongue.

There be six ways appointed by the best learned men for the
learning of tongues and increase of eloquence, as:

[10] 1570: ill.
[11] 1570: be. But Mayor's emendation to *he* makes sense out of what is
otherwise a garbled couplet.
[12] Taken away.       [13] 1570: in.

## The Ready Way to the Latin Tongue

1. *Translatio linguarum*
2. *Paraphrasis*
3. *Metaphrasis*
4. *Epitome*
5. *Imitatio*
6. *Declamatio.*

All these be used and commended, but in order and for respects, as person, ability, place, and time shall require. The five last be fitter for the master than the scholar, for men than for children, for the universities rather than for grammar schools; yet nevertheless, which is fittest in mine opinion for our school, and which is either wholly to be refused or partly to be used for our purpose I will, by good authority and some reason, I trust, particularly of every one and largely enough of them all, declare orderly unto you.

## Translatio linguarum

Translation is easy in the beginning for the scholar and bringeth also [14] much learning and great judgment to the master. It is most common and most commendable of all other exercises for youth. Most common, for all your constructions in grammar schools be nothing else but translations; but because they be not double translations, as I do require, they bring forth but simple and single commodity, and because also they lack the daily use of writing, which is the only thing that breedeth deep root, both in the wit for good understanding and in the memory for sure keeping of all that is learned. Most commendable also, and that by the judgment of all authors which entreat [15] of these exercises. Tully in the person of Lucius Crassus, whom he maketh his example of eloquence and true judgment in learning, doth not only praise specially and choose this way of translation for a young man, but doth also discommend and

[14] 1571; 1570: all.    [15] Treat.

refuse his own former wont in exercising *paraphrasin* and *metaphrasin*.[16] *Paraphrasis* is to take some eloquent oration, or some notable commonplace in Latin, and express it with other words. *Metaphrasis* is to take some notable place out of a good poet and turn the same sense into meter or into other words in prose. Crassus, or rather Tully, doth mislike both these ways because the author, either orator or poet, had chosen out before the fittest words and aptest composition for that matter, and so he, in seeking other, was driven to use the worse.

Quintilian also preferreth translation before all other exercises; yet, having a lust to dissent from Tully (as he doth in very many places, if a man read his rhetoric over advisedly, and that rather of an envious mind than of any just cause), doth greatly commend *paraphrasis,* crossing spitefully Tully's judgment in refusing the same,[17] and so do Ramus and Talaeus [18] even at this day in France, too. But such singularity in dissenting from the best men's judgments, in liking only their own opinions, is much misliked of all them that join with learning discretion and wisdom. For he that can neither like Aristotle in logic and philosophy nor Tully in rhetoric and eloquence will, from these steps, likely enough presume by like pride to mount higher to the misliking of greater matters; that is, either in religion to have a dissentious head or in the commonwealth to have a factious heart, as I knew one, a student in Cambridge, who, for a singularity, began first to dissent in the schools from Aristotle and soon after became a perverse Arian, against Christ and all true religion, and studied diligently Origen, Basileus, and St. Jerome only to glean out of their works the pernicious heresies of Celsus, Eunomius, and Helvidius, whereby the church of Christ was so poisoned withal.

---

[16] *De oratore,* I.xxxiv.154–155.    [17] *Institutio oratoria,* X.v.3–8.
[18] Pierre de la Ramée (Petrus Ramus) and Omer Talon (Talaeus), reformers of dialetical and rhetorical studies who favored a clear separation of the two arts.

## The Ready Way to the Latin Tongue

But to leave these high points of divinity, surely in this quiet and harmless controversy for the liking or misliking of *paraphrasis* for a young scholar, even as far as Tully goeth beyond Quintilian, Ramus, and Talaeus in perfect eloquence, even so much, by mine opinion, come they behind Tully for true judgment in teaching the same.

Plinius Secundus, a wise senator, of great experience, excellently learned himself, a liberal patron of learned men, and the purest writer, in mine opinion, of all his age (I except not Suetonius, his two schoolmasters Quintilian and Tacitus, nor yet his most learned uncle, the elder Plinius), doth express in an epistle to his friend Fuscus many good ways for order in study, but he beginneth with translation and preferreth it to all the rest. And because his words be notable, I will recite them:

*Utile in primis, ut multi praecipiunt, ex Graeco in Latinum et ex Latino vertere in Graecum: quo genere exercitationis proprietas splendorque verborum, apta structura sententiarum, figurarum copia et explicandi vis colligitur. Praeterea imitatione optimorum facultas similia inveniendi paratur: et quae legentem fefellissent, transferentem fugere non possunt. Intelligentia ex hoc et judicium acquiritur.*[19]

Ye perceive how Pliny teacheth that by this exercise of double translating is learned easily, sensibly, by little and little, not only all the hard congruities of grammar, the choice of aptest words, the right framing of words and sentences, comeliness of

[19] *Letters,* VII.ix.1 (erroneously cited in marginal note as VI.vii): "It is a very advantageous practice (and what many recommend) to translate either from Greek into Latin, or from Latin into Greek. By this sort of exercise one acquires noble and proper expressions, [suitable arrangement of sentences,] variety of figures, and a forcible turn of exposition. Besides, to imitate the most approved authors, gives one aptitude to invent after their manner, and at the same time, things which you might have overlooked in reading cannot escape you in translating: and this method will open your understanding and improve your judgment." Reprinted by permission of the publishers and the Loeb Classical Library from Pliny, *Letters,* trans. William Melmoth, rev. W. M. L. Hutchinson, II (Cambridge, Mass: Harvard University Press, 1958), 21–23.

figures and forms, fit for every matter and proper for every tongue, but that which is greater also, in marking daily and following diligently thus the steps of the best authors, like invention of arguments, like order in disposition, like utterance in elocution is easily gathered up, whereby your scholar shall be brought not only to like eloquence but also to all true understanding and right judgment, both for writing and speaking. And where Dionysius Halicarnasseus hath written two excellent books, the one *De delectu optimorum verborum,* the which I fear is lost, the other, of the right framing of words and sentences,[20] which doth remain yet in Greek, to the great profit of all them that truly study for eloquence, yet this way of double translating shall bring the whole profit of both these books to a diligent scholar, and that easily and pleasantly both for fit choice of words and apt composition of sentences. And by these authorities and reasons am I moved to think this way of double translating, either only or chiefly, to be fittest for the speedy and perfect attaining of any tongue. And for speedy attaining, I durst venture a good wager, if a scholar in whom is aptness, love, diligence, and constancy would but translate after this sort one little book in Tully, as *De senectute,* with two epistles, the first *Ad Quintum fratrem,* the other *Ad Lentulum* (the last, save one, in the first book)—that scholar, I say, should come to a better knowledge in the Latin tongue than the most part do that spend four or five years in tossing all the rules of grammar in common schools. Indeed this one book with these two epistles is not sufficient to afford all Latin words (which is not necessary for a young scholar to know), but it is able to furnish him fully for all points of grammar, with the right placing, ordering, and use of words in all kind of matter. And why not? For it is read that Dio Prusaeus, that wise philosopher and excellent orator of all his time, did come to the great learning

[20] Περὶ συνθέσεως ὀνομάτων (1st century B.C.), a treatise on the selection and ordering of diction in the various styles of oratory.

## The Ready Way to the Latin Tongue

and utterance that was in him by reading and following only two books, *Phaedon Platonis* and Demosthenes' most notable oration Περί παραπρεσβείας.[21] And a better and nearer example herein may be our most noble Queen Elizabeth, who never took yet Greek nor Latin grammar in her hand after the first declining of a noun and a verb, but only by this double translating of Demosthenes and Isocrates daily without missing every forenoon, and likewise some part of Tully every afternoon, for the space of a year or two, hath attained to such a perfect understanding in both the tongues and to such a ready utterance of the Latin, and that with such a judgment as they be few in number in both the universities, or elsewhere in England, that be in both tongues comparable with Her Majesty. And to conclude in a short room [22] the commodities of double translation, surely the mind by daily marking, first, the cause and matter; then, the words and phrases; next, the order and composition; after, the reason and arguments; then, the forms and figures of both the tongues; lastly, the measure and compass of every sentence, must needs by little and little draw unto it the like shape of eloquence as the author doth use which is read.

And thus much for double translation.

### Paraphrasis

*Paraphrasis*, the second point, is not only to express at large with more words, but to strive and contend (as Quintilian saith) [23] to translate the best Latin authors into other Latin words, as many or thereabouts.

This way of exercise was used first by Caius Carbo and taken up for a while by Lucius Crassus, but soon after, upon due proof thereof, rejected justly by Crassus and Cicero; yet allowed and made sterling again by Marcus Quintilian; nevertheless shortly after, by better assay, disallowed of his own scholar

[21] Philostratus, *Lives of the Sophists*, I.vii.488.
[22] Space.     [23] *Institutio oratoria*, X.v.4–8.

Plinius Secundus, who termeth it rightly thus: *Audax conten-tio.*[24] It is a bold comparison indeed to think to say better than that is best. Such turning of the best into worse is much like the turning of good wine out of a fair, sweet flagon of silver into a foul, musty bottle of leather, or to turn pure gold and silver into foul brass and copper.

Such kind of *paraphrasis,* in turning, chopping, and changing the best to worse, either in the mint or schools (though Master Broke [25] and Quintilian both say the contrary), is much mis-liked of the best and wisest men. I can better allow another kind of *paraphrasis:* to turn rude and barbarous into proper and eloquent, which nevertheless is an exercise not fit for a scholar but for a perfect master, who in plenty hath good choice, in *copia* [26] hath right judgment and grounded skill, as did appear to be in Sebastian Castalio, in translating Kempis' book *De imitando Christi.*[27]

But to follow Quintilianus' advice for *paraphrasis* were even to take pain to seek the worse and fouler way when the plain and fairer is occupied before your eyes.

The old and best authors that ever wrote were content, if occasion required to speak twice of one matter, not to change the words, but ῥητῶς, that is, word for word to express it again. For they thought that a matter well expressed with fit words and apt composition was not to be altered, but liking it well theirselves, they thought it also would be well allowed of others.

A schoolmaster (such one as I require) knoweth that I say true.

[24] *Letters,* VII.ix.4: "A bold contest" with one's model.
[25] Thomas Broke (fl. 1550), who appended to William Huycke's transla-tion of *Geneva. The forme of common praiers used in the Churches of Geneva* (London, 1550) several graces, the first and last of which are respectively paraphrases of the Ten Commandments and the Lord's Prayer (sigs. 204r–v, 208r–209r).
[26] Abundance of vocabulary.
[27] Sébastien Castalion's paraphrase into "more eloquent" Latin of Thomas à Kempis' *De imitatione Christi* was published at Basel in 1563.

## The Ready Way to the Latin Tongue

He readeth in Homer, almost in every book, and specially in *secundo et nono Iliados*, not only some verses, but whole leaves, not to be altered with new, but to be uttered with the old selfsame words.

He knoweth that Xenophon, writing twice of Agesilaus, once in his *Life*, again in the *History of the Greeks*, in one matter keepeth always the selfsame words. He doth the like, speaking of Socrates, both in the beginning of his *Apology* and in the last end of Ἀπομνημονευμάτων.[28]

Demosthenes also in fourth *Philippica* doth borrow his own words uttered before in his oration *De Chersoneso*. He doth the like, and that more at large, in his orations against Androtion and Timocrates.[29]

In Latin also, Cicero in some places, and Virgil in more, do repeat one matter with the selfsame words. These excellent authors did thus, not for lack of words, but by judgment and skill, whatsoever other more curious and less skillful do think, write, and do.

*Paraphrasis* nevertheless hath good place in learning, but not, by mine opinion, for any scholar, but is only to be left to a perfect master either to expound openly a good author withal or to compare privately, for his own exercise, how some notable place of an excellent author may be uttered with other fit words. But if ye alter also the composition, form, and order, then that is not *paraphrasis* but *imitatio*, as I will fully declare in fitter place.

The scholar shall win nothing by *paraphrasis* but only, if we

[28] For Xenophon's practice of using entire passages again with little or no alteration, compare his accounts of Agesilaus' campaign against the Persians in 396 B.C. in *Agesilaus*, I.6–35, with that in the *History of the Greeks* (Ἑλληνικά), III.iv.2–25 *passim*, and of Hermogenes' dialogue with Socrates in *Apology*, 2–6, with *Memorabilia*, IV.viii.4–7.

[29] *Fourth Philippic*, 11–27 and 55–70 are repeated from *On the Chersonese*, 38–51 and 56–69; *Timocrates*, 160–168, 172–186, from *Androtion*, 47–56, 65–78. The fact that modern editors doubt Demosthenes' authorship of the *Fourth Philippic* somewhat vitiates Ascham's first example.

## The Schoolmaster

may believe Tully, to choose worse words, to place them out of order, to fear overmuch the judgment of the master, to mislike overmuch the hardness of learning, and by use to gather up faults which hardly will be left off again.

The master, in teaching it, shall rather increase his own labor than his scholar's profit, for when the scholar shall bring unto his master a piece of Tully or Caesar turned into other Latin, then must the master come to Quintilian's goodly lesson *de emendatione,* which (as he saith) is the most profitable part of teaching,[30] but not in mine opinion, and namely for youth in grammar schools. For the master now taketh double pains, first, to mark what is amiss, again, to invent what may be said better. And here, perchance, a very good master may easily both deceive himself and lead his scholar into error.

It requireth greater learning and deeper judgment than is to be hoped for at any schoolmaster's hand; that is, to be able always learnedly and perfectly

> *Mutare quod ineptum est;*
> *Transmutare quod perversum est;*
> *Replere quod deest;*
> *Detrahere quod obest;*
> *Expungere quod inane est.*[31]

And that which requireth more skill and deeper consideration:

> *Premere tumentia;*
> *Extollere humilia;*
> *Astringere luxuriantia;*
> *Componere dissoluta.*[32]

[30] *Institutio oratoria,* X.iv.1.

[31] "To alter what is unsuitable; change what is wrong; make good what is wanting; remove what impedes; blot out what is useless."

[32] "To suppress bombast, elevate the common, check excess, . . . set the disarrayed in order" (Quintilian, *Institutio oratoria,* X.iv.1).

## The Ready Way to the Latin Tongue

The master may here only stumble and perchance fall in teaching, to the marring and maiming [33] of the scholar in learning, when it is a matter of much reading, of great learning and tried judgment, to make true difference betwixt

*Sublime et tumidum;*
*Grande et immodicum;*
*Decorum et ineptum;*
*Perfectum et nimium.*[34]

Some men of our time, counted perfect masters of eloquence (in their own opinion the best, in other men's judgments very good) as Omphalius [35] everywhere, Sadoletus [36] in many places, yea, also my friend Osorius, namely in his epistle to the Queen and in his whole book *De justitia,*[37] have so overreached themselves in making true difference in the points afore rehearsed as though they had been brought up in some school in Asia to learn to decline [38] rather than in Athens with Plato, Aristotle, and Demosthenes (from whence Tully fetched his eloquence) to understand what in every matter to be spoken or written on is, in very deed, *nimium, satis, parum;* [39] that is for to say, to all considerations, *decorum,* which, as it is the hardest point in all learning, so is it the fairest and only mark that scholars in all

[33] 1570: mayning.

[34] "Sublime and pompous; elevated and unbridled; seemly and tasteless; complete and excessive."

[35] Jakob Omphalius (1500–1567), German lawyer and humanist who wrote *De elocutionis imitatione ac apparatu liber unus* (Paris, 1537).

[36] Cardinal Jacopo Sadoleto (1477–1547), Italian humanist and author of a celebrated treatise on education, *De liberis recte instituendis* (Venice, 1533).

[37] Jeronimo Osorio da Fonseca (1506–1580), Portuguese bishop and historian, whose *Epistola . . . ad serenissimam Elisabetam Angliae reginam* (Louvain, 1563), urging the Queen to restore Catholicism in England, involved him in a polemical exchange over the reformed religion with Ascham's friend Walter Haddon.

[38] Declaim.       [39] "Too much, sufficient, too little."

The Schoolmaster

their study must always shoot at if they purpose another day to be either sound in religion or wise and discreet in any vocation of the commonwealth.

Again, in the lowest degree, it is no low point of learning and judgment for a schoolmaster to make true difference betwixt

*Humile et depressum;*
*Lene et remissum;*
*Siccum et aridum;*
*Exile et macrum;*
*Inaffectatum et neglectum.*[40]

In these points some, loving Melanchthon well, as he was well worthy, but yet not considering well nor wisely how he of nature, and all his life and study by judgment, was wholly spent in *genere disciplinabili,* that is, in teaching, reading, and expounding plainly and aptly school matters, and therefore employed thereunto a fit, sensible, and calm kind of speaking and writing—some, I say, with very well loving [41] but not with very well weighing Melanchthon's doings, do frame themselves a style cold, lean, and weak, though the matter be never so warm and earnest, not much unlike unto one that had a pleasure in a rough, rainy winter day to clothe himself with nothing else but a demi-buckram [42] cassock, plain without pleats and single without lining, which will neither bear off wind nor weather, nor yet keep out the sun in any hot day.

Some suppose (and that by good reason) that Melanchthon himself came to this low kind of writing by using overmuch *paraphrasis* in reading; for studying thereby to make everything straight and easy, in smoothing and planing all things too much, never leaveth (while the sense itself be left) both loose and lazy. And some of those *paraphrases* of Melanchthon be set out

[40] "Plain and low; smooth and slack; dry and arid; measured and meager; unaffected and careless."
[41] 1570: living.    [42] A coarse, stiffened linen fabric.

92

# The Ready Way to the Latin Tongue

in print, as *Pro Archia poeta* and *Marco Marcello*.[43] But a scholar, by mine opinion, is better occupied in playing or sleeping than in spending time, not only vainly but also harmfully, in such a kind of exercise.

If a master would have a perfect example to follow, how in *genere sublimi* to avoid *nimium*, or in *mediocri* to attain *satis*, or in *humili* to eschew *parum*, let him read diligently for the first *Secundam Philippicam*, for the mean *De natura deorum*, and for the lowest *Partitiones*.[44] Or if in another tongue ye look for like example, in like perfection for all those three degrees, read *Pro Ctesiphonte, Ad Leptinem*, and *Contra Olympiodorum*,[45] and what wit, art, and diligence is able to afford ye shall plainly see.

For our time, the odd [46] man to perform all three perfectly, whatsoever he doth, and to know the way to do them skillfully, whensoever he list, is, in my poor opinion, Joannes Sturmius.

He also counseleth all scholars to beware of *paraphrasis*, except it be from worse to better, from rude and barbarous to proper and pure Latin, and yet no man to exercise that neither, except such one as is already furnished with plenty of learning and grounded with steadfast judgment before.[47]

All these faults that thus many wise men do find with the

---

[43] Both orations of Cicero.

[44] Ascham is recommending three Ciceronian models for learning how to avoid the main danger that awaits the unwary in each of the three rhetorical styles (*genera*). Hence, to avoid excess (*nimium*) in the high (*sublimi*) style, he should read Cicero's *Second Philippic* against Antony; to attain what is sufficient (*satis*) in the middle (*mediocri*) style, his *De natura deorum;* to eschew what is too little (*parum*) in the low (*humili*) style, the *De partitione oratoria.*

[45] All orations by Demosthenes.       [46] Only.

[47] *De imitatione oratoria*, sig. C8v: *Paraphrasibus bonorum orationes in eadem lingua explicando dilatare, aut aliis verbis commutare non laudo: quicquid enim substituetur fiet deterius. Nam boni oratoris est, et fuit illis aetatibus omnium oratorum, ita scribere: ut nihil additum, aut abstractum, aut transpositum potuisset effectum opus facere melius.*

exercise of *paraphrasis* in turning the best Latin into other as good as they can, that is, ye may be sure, into a great deal worse than it was, both in right choice for propriety and true placing for good order, is committed also commonly in all common schools by the schoolmasters in tossing and troubling young wits (as I said in the beginning) with that butcherly fear in making of Latins.

Therefore, in place of Latins for young scholars and of *paraphrasis* for the masters, I would have double translation specially used. For in double translating a perfect piece of Tully or Caesar, neither the scholar in learning nor the master in teaching can err. A true touchstone, a sure metwand[48] lieth before both their eyes. For all right congruity, propriety of words, order in sentences, the right imitation—to invent good matter, to dispose it in good order, to confirm it with good reason, to express any purpose fitly and orderly—is learned thus both easily and perfectly. Yea, to miss sometime in this kind of translation bringeth more profit than to hit right either in *paraphrasis* or making of Latins. For though ye say well in a Latin making or in a *paraphrasis,* yet you being but in doubt and uncertain whether ye say well or no, ye gather and lay up in memory no sure fruit of learning thereby, but if ye fault in translation, ye are easily taught how perfectly to amend it, and so, well warned how after to eschew all such faults again.

*Paraphrasis* therefore, by mine opinion, is not meet for grammar schools nor yet very fit for young men in the university until study and time have bred in them perfect learning and steadfast judgment.

There is a kind of *paraphrasis* which may be used without all hurt to much profit, but it serveth only the Greek and not the Latin nor no other tongue; as, to alter *linguam Ionicam aut Doricam* into *meram Atticam.*[49] A notable example there is left

[48] Measuring rod; hence, a standard of judgment.
[49] The Ionic or Doric dialect into pure Attic; that is, into the speech of Athens.

unto us by a notable learned man, Dionysius Halicarnasseus, who in his book Περὶ συντάξεος doth translate the goodly story of Candaules and Gyges in first *Herodoti* out of *Ionica lingua* into *Atticam*.[50] Read the place, and ye shall take both pleasure and profit in conference [51] of it. A man that is exercised in reading Thucydides, Xenophon, Plato, and Demosthenes, in using to turn like places of Herodotus after like sort, should shortly come to such a knowledge in understanding, speaking, and writing the Greek tongue as few or none hath yet attained in England. The like exercise out of *Dorica lingua* may be also used, if a man take that little book of Plato, *Timaeus Locrus de animo et natura*, which is written *Dorice*, and turn it into such Greek as Plato useth in other works.[52] The book is but two leaves, and the labor would be but two weeks; but surely the profit for easy understanding and true writing the Greek tongue would countervail with [53] the toil that some men taketh in otherwise coldly reading that tongue two years.

And yet for the Latin tongue, and for the exercise of *paraphrasis* in those places of Latin that cannot be bettered, if some young man, excellent of wit, courageous in will, lusty of nature, and desirous to contend even with the best Latin to better it, if he can, surely I commend his forwardness, and for his better instruction therein I will set before him as notable an example of *paraphrasis* as is in record of learning. Cicero himself doth contend in two sundry places to express one matter with diverse words, and that is *paraphrasis,* saith Quintilian. The matter, I suppose, is taken out of Panaetius,[54] and therefore, being translated out of Greek at divers times, is uttered for his purpose

[50] Actually, Dionysius Halicarnasseus, Περὶ συνθέσεως, iii.24.

[51] Comparing.

[52] The tract referred to, often printed in editions of Plato, is the *De anima mundi et natura,* a work attributed to one Timaeus of Locri but probably an epitome of a part of Plato's own dialogue *Timaeus.*

[53] Counterbalance.

[54] Greek Stoic philosopher (2nd century B.C.) whose treatise *On Duties* was the principal source of ideas for Cicero's *De officiis.*

## The Schoolmaster

with divers words and forms; which kind of exercise, for perfect learned men, is very profitable.

### 2. *De finibus*

a. *Homo enim rationem habet a natura menti datam, quae, causas rerum et consecutiones videt, et similitudines transfert, et disjuncta conjungit, et cum praesentibus futura copulat, omnemque complectitur vitae consequentis statum.* b. *Eademque ratio facit hominem hominum appetentem, cumque his, natura, et sermone et usu congruentem: ut profectus a caritate domesticorum ac suorum, currat longius, et se implicet, primo civium, deinde omnium mortalium societati: utque non sibi soli se natum meminerit, sed patriae, sed suis, ut exigua pars ipsi relinquatur.* c. *Et quoniam eadem natura cupiditatem ingenuit homini veri inveniendi, quod facillime apparet, cum vacui curis, etiam quid in coelo fiat, scire avemus, etc.*[55]

### 1. *Officiorum*

a. *Homo autem, qui rationis est particeps, per quam consequentia cernit, et causas rerum videt, earumque progressus, et*

[55] In this and the following quotation Ascham's Latin text varies in several respects from that in modern critical editions of Cicero. The Loeb translation of this passage from *De finibus*, II.xiv.45–46, reads as follows: "For among the many points of difference between man and the lower animals, the greatest difference is that Nature has bestowed on man the gift of Reason, of an active, vigorous intelligence, able to prosecute several trains of thought with great swiftness at the same time, and having, so to speak, a keen scent to discern the sequence of causes and effects, to draw analogies, combine things separate, connect the future with the present, and survey the entire field of the subsequent course of life. It is Reason moreover that has inspired man with a relish for his kind; she has produced conformity of character, of language and of habit; she has prompted the individual, starting from friendship and from family affection, to expand his interests, forming social ties first with his fellow-citizens and later with all mankind. She reminds him that, as Plato puts it in his letter to Archytas, man was not born for self alone, but for country and for kindred, claims that leave but a small part of him for himself. Nature has also engendered in mankind the desire of contemplating truth. This is most clearly manifested in our hours of leisure; when our minds are at ease we are eager to acquire knowledge even of the movements of the heavenly bodies." Reprinted by permission of the publishers and the Loeb Classical Library from Cicero, *De finibus bonorum et malorum*, trans. H. Rackham (Cambridge, Mass.: Harvard University Press, 1951), pp. 133–135.

*quasi antecessiones non ignorat, similitudines comparat, rebusque praesentibus adjungit, atque annectit futuras, facile totius vitae cursum videt, ad eamque degendam praeparat res necessarias. b. Eademque natura vi rationis hominem conciliat homini, et ad orationis, et ad vitae societatem: ingeneratque imprimis praecipuum quendam amorem in eos, qui procreati sunt, impellitque ut hominum caetus et celebrari inter se, et sibi obediri velit, ob easque causas, studeat parare ea, quae suppeditent ad cultum et ad victum, nec sibi soli, sed conjugi, liberis, caeterisque quos charos habeat, tuerique debeat. c. Quae cura exsuscitat etiam animos, et majores ad rem gerendam facit: imprimisque hominis est propria veri inquisitio atque investigatio: ita cum sumus necessariis negotiis curisque vacui, tum avemus aliquid videre, audire, addiscere, cognitionemque rerum mirabilium, etc.*[56]

The conference of these two places, containing so excellent a piece of learning as this is, expressed by so worthy a wit as Tully's was, must needs bring great pleasure and profit to him

---

[56] "While man—because he is endowed with reason, by which he comprehends the chain of consequences, perceives the causes of things, understands the relation of cause to effect and of effect to cause, draws analogies, and connects and associates the present and the future—easily surveys the course of his whole life and makes the necessary preparations for its conduct.

"Nature likewise by the power of reason associates man with man in the common bonds of speech and life; she implants in him above all, I may say, a strangely tender love for his offspring. She also prompts men to meet in companies, to form public assemblies and to take part in them themselves; and she further dictates, as a consequence of this, the effort on man's part to provide a store of things that minister to his comforts and wants—and not for himself alone, but for his wife and children and the others whom he holds dear and for whom he ought to provide; and this responsibility also stimulates his courage and makes it stronger for the active duties of life.

"Above all, the search after truth and its eager pursuit are peculiar to man. And so, when we have leisure from the demands of business cares, we are eager to see, to hear, to learn something new, and we esteem a desire to know the secrets or wonders of creation as indispensable to a happy life." Reprinted by permission of the publishers and the Loeb Classical Library from Cicero, *De officiis* (I.iv.11–13), trans. Walter Miller (Cambridge, Mass.: Harvard University Press, 1951), pp. 13–15.

# The Schoolmaster

that maketh true count of learning and honesty. But if we had the Greek author, the first pattern of all, and thereby to see how Tully's wit did work at divers times, how out of one excellent image might be framed two other, one in face and favor but somewhat differing in form, figure, and color, surely such a piece of workmanship compared with the pattern itself would better please the eyes [57] of honest, wise, and learned minds than two of the fairest Venuses that ever Apelles made.

And thus much for all kind of *paraphrasis,* fit or unfit, for scholars or other, as I am led to think not only by mine own experience but chiefly by the authority and judgment of those whom I myself would gladliest follow and do counsel all mine to do the same, not contending with any other that will otherwise either think or do.

## *Metaphrasis*

This kind of exercise is all one with *paraphrasis,* save it is out of verse either into prose or into some other kind of meter, or else out of prose into verse, which was Socrates' exercise and pastime (as Plato reporteth) when he was in prison, to translate Aesop's *Fables* into verse.[58] Quintilian doth greatly praise also this exercise, but because Tully doth disallow it in young men,[59] by mine opinion it were not well to use it [in] [60] grammar schools even for the selfsame causes that be recited against *paraphrasis.* And therefore, for the use, or misuse, of it the same is to be thought that is spoken of *paraphrasis* before. This was Sulpitius' exercise, and he, gathering up thereby a poetical kind of talk, is justly named of Cicero *grandis et tragicus orator;* which I think is spoken not for his praise but for other men's warning to eschew the like fault.[61] Yet nevertheless, if our schoolmaster for his own instruction be desirous to see a perfect

[57] 1570: ease.    [58] *Phaedo,* 60D.
[59] Quintilian, *Institutio oratoria,* X.v.4; Cicero, *De oratore,* I.xxxiv.154.
[60] *In* from 1571 edition.    [61] *Brutus,* lv.203.

98

## The Ready Way to the Latin Tongue

example hereof, I will recite one which I think no man is so bold, will say that he can amend it, and that is Chryses the priest's oration to the Greeks in the beginning of Homer's *Ilias*, turned excellently into prose by Socrates himself, and that advisedly and purposely for other to follow; and therefore he calleth this exercise in the same place μίμησις, that is, *imitatio*, which is most true, but in this book, for teaching's sake, I will name it *metaphrasis*, retaining the word that all teachers in this case do use.

Homerus 1. Ἰλίαδ

'Ο γὰρ ἦλθε θοὰς ἐπὶ νῆας 'Αχαιῶν,
λυσόμενός τε θύγατρα φέρων τ' ἀπερείσι' ἄποινα·
στέμματ' ἔχων ἐν χερσὶν ἐκηβόλου 'Απόλλωνος,
χρυσέῳ ἀνὰ σκήπτρῳ· καὶ ἐλίσσετο πάντας 'Αχαιούς.
'Ατρεΐδα δὲ μάλιστα δύω, κοσμήτορε λαῶν.
'Ατρεΐδαι τε καὶ ἄλλοι ἐϋκνήμειδες 'Αχαιοί,
ὑμῖν μὲν θεοὶ δοῖεν 'Ολύμπια δώματ' ἔχοντες,
ἐκπέρσαι Πριάμοιο πόλιν, ἐϋ δ' οἴκαδ' ἱκέσθαι.
παῖδα δ' ἐμοὶ λύσατε φίλην, τὰ δ' ἄποινα δέχεσθε,
ἁζόμενοι Διὸς υἱὸν ἐκηβόλον 'Απόλλωνα.

"Ενθ' ἄλλοι μὲν πάντες ἐπευφήμησαν 'Αχαιοὶ
αἰδεῖσθαί θ' ἱερῆα, καὶ ἀγλαὰ δέχθαι ἄποινα.

'Αλλ' οὐκ 'Ατρεΐδῃ 'Αγαμέμνονι ἥνδανε θυμῷ,
ἀλλὰ κακῶς ἀφίει, κρατερὸν δ' ἐπὶ μῦθον ἔτελλε·
μή σε γέρων κοίλησιν ἐγὼ παρὰ νηυσὶ κικείω,
ἢ νῦν δηθύνοντα, ἢ ὕστερον αὖτις ἰόντα,
μή νύ τοι οὐ χραίσμῃ σκῆπτρον καὶ στέμμα θεοῖο.
τὴν δ' ἐγὼ οὐ λύσω, πρίν μιν καὶ γῆρας ἔπεισιν,
ἡμετέρῳ ἐνὶ οἴκῳ, ἐν 'Αργεῖ τηλόθι πάτρης
'ιστὸν ἐποιχομένην καὶ ἐμὸν λέχος ἀντιόωσαν.
ἀλλ' ἴθι, μή μ' ἐρέθιζε, σαώτερος ὥς κε νέηαι.

"Ως ἔφατ', ἔδδεισεν δ' ὁ γέρων, καὶ ἐπείθετο μύθῳ.
βῆ δ' ἀκέων παρὰ θῖνα πολυφλοίσβοιο θαλάσσης.
πολλὰ δ' ἔπειτ' ἀπάνευθε κιὼν ἠρᾶθ' ὁ γεραιὸς
'Απόλλωνι ἄνακτι, τὸν ἠΰκομος τέκε Λητώ.

# The Schoolmaster

Κλῦθί μευ ἀργυρότοξ', ὅσ Χρύσην ἀμφιβέβηκας,
Κίλλαν τε ζαθέην, Τενέδοιό τε ἶφι ἀνάσσεις
Σμινθεῦ, εἴ ποτέ τοι χαρίεντ' ἐπὶ νηὸν ἔρεψα,
ἢ εἰ δή ποτέ τοι κατὰ πίονα μηρί' ἔκηα
ταύρων, ἠδ' αἰγῶν, τόδε μοι κρήηνον ἐέλδωρ.
τίσειαν Δαναοὶ ἐμὰ δάκρυα σοῖσι βέλεσσιν.[62]

Socrates in 3. *De republica* saith thus:

Φράσω δὲ ἄνευ μέτρου, οὐ γάρ εἰμι ποιητικός.
ἦλθεν ὁ Χρύσησ, τῆς τε θυγατρὸς λύτρα φέρων, καὶ ἱκέτης τῶν 'Αχαιῶν, μάλιστα δὲ
τῶν βασιλέων· καὶ ηὔχετο, ἐκείνοις μὲν τοὺς θεοὺς δοῦναι 'ελόντας τὴν Τροίαν, αὐτοὺς
σωθῆαι, τὴν τε θυγατέρα ὃι αὐτῷ λῦσαι, δεξαμένους ἄποινα, καὶ τὸν θεὸν αἰδεσθέντας.

[62] "For he had come to the swift ships of the Achaeans to free his
daughter, and he bore with him ransom past counting; and in his hands he
held the fillets of Apollo, that smiteth afar, on a staff of gold, and he made
prayer to all the Achaeans, but most of all to the two sons of Atreus, the
marshallers of the host: 'Ye sons of Atreus, and ye other well-greaved
Achaeans, to you may the gods who have homes upon Olympus grant that
ye sack the city of Priam, and return safe to your homes; but my dear
child do ye set free for me, and accept the ransom out of awe for the son
of Zeus, Apollo, that smiteth afar.'
"Then all the rest of the Achaeans shouted assent, bidding reverence the
priest and accept the glorious ransom, yet the thing pleased not the heart
of Agamemnon, son of Atreus, but he sent him away harshly, and laid
upon him a stern command: 'Let me not find thee, old man, by the hollow
ships, either tarrying now or coming back hereafter, lest thy staff and the
fillet of the god protect thee not. But her will I not set free: ere that shall
old age come upon her in our house, in Argos, far from her country, as she
walks to and fro before the loom and tends my couch. Nay, get thee gone;
anger me not, that so thou mayest go the safer.'
"So he spake, and the old man was seized with fear and hearkened to
his word. Forth he went in silence along the shore of the loud-resounding
sea, and earnestly thereafter, when he had gone apart, did the old man
pray to the prince, Apollo, whom fair-haired Leto bare: 'Hear me, thou of
the silver bow, who dost stand over Chryse and holy Cilla, and dost rule
mightily over Tenedos, thou Sminthian, if ever I roofed over a shrine to
thy pleasing, or if ever I burned to thee fat thigh-pieces of bulls or goats,
fulfill thou for me this prayer: let the Danaans pay for my tears by thy
shafts' " (ll. 12–42). Reprinted by permission of the publishers and the
Loeb Classical Library from Homer, *The Iliad*, trans. A. T. Murray, I
(Cambridge, Mass.: Harvard University Press, 1960), 3–7.

100

# The Ready Way to the Latin Tongue

τοιαῦτα δὲ εἰπόντος αὐτοῦ, οἱ μὲν ἄλλοι ἐσέβοντο καὶ συνῄνουν. ὁ δὲ ᾿Αγαμέμνων ἠγρίαινεν, ἐντελλόμενος νῦν τ᾿ ἀπιέναι, καὶ αὖθις μὴ ἐλθεῖν, μὴ αὐτῷ τό, τε σκῆπτρον καὶ τὰ τοῦ θεοῦ στέμματα οὐκ ἐπαρκέσοι. πρὶν δὲ λυθῆναι αὐτοῦ θυγατέρα, ἐν ῎Αργει ἔφη γηράσειν μετὰ οὗ. ἀπιέναι δ᾿ ἐκέλευε, καὶ μὴ ἐρεθίζειν, ἵνα σῶς οἴκαδα ἔλθοι. ὁ δὲ πρεσβύτης ἀκούσασ, ἐδεισέ τε καὶ ἀπῄει σιγῇ. ἀποχωρήσασ δὲ ἐκ τοῦ στρατοπέδου, πολλὰ τῷ ᾿Απόλλωνι ηὔχετο᾿ τάς τε ἐπωνυμίας τοῦ θεοῦ ἀνακαλῶν, καὶ ὑπομιμνήσκων καὶ ἀπαιτῶν, εἴ τι πώποτε ἢ ἐν ναῶν οἰκοδομήσεσιν, ἢ ἐν ἱερῶν θυσίαις κεχαρισμένον δωρήσαιτο, ὧν δὴ χάριν κατεύχετο τῖσαι τοὺς ᾿Αχαιοὺς τὰ ἃ δάκρυα τοῖς, ἐκείνου βέλεσιν.[63]

To compare Homer and Plato together, two wonders of nature and art for wit and eloquence, is most pleasant and profitable for a man of ripe judgment. Plato's turning of Homer in this place doth not ride aloft in poetical terms but goeth low and soft on foot, as prose and *pedestris oratio* [64] should do. If Sulpitius had had Plato's consideration in right using this exercise, he had not deserved the name of *tragicus orator,* who should rather have studied to express *vim Demosthenis* than *furorem poetae,*[65] how good soever he was whom he did follow. And therefore would I have our schoolmaster weigh well

[63] "Chryses came with the ransom of his daughter and as a suppliant of the Achaeans but chiefly of the kings . . . and prayed that to them the gods should grant to take Troy and come safely home, but that they should accept the ransom and release his daughter, out of reverence for the god; and when he had thus spoken the others were of reverent mind and approved, but Agamemnon was angry and bade him depart and not come again lest the sceptre and the fillets of the god should not avail him. And ere his daughter should be released, he said, she would grow old in Argos with himself, and he ordered him to be off and not vex him if he wished to get home safe. And the old man on hearing this was frightened and departed in silence, and having gone apart from the camp he prayed at length to Apollo, invoking the appellations of the god, and reminding him of and asking requital for any of his gifts that had found favour whether in the building of temples or the sacrifice of victims. In return for these things he prayed that the Achaeans should suffer for his tears by the god's shafts" (393D–394A). Reprinted by permission of the publishers and the Loeb Classical Library from Plato, *The Republic,* trans. Paul Shorey, I (Cambridge, Mass.: Harvard University Press, 1963), 229–231.

[64] Ordinary speech.

[65] The force of Demosthenes than the transport of the poet.

together Homer and Plato and mark diligently these four points: what is kept, what is added, what is left out, what is changed either in choice of words or form of sentences; which four points be the right tools to handle like a workman this kind of work, as our scholar shall better understand when he hath been a good while in the university, to which time and place I chiefly remit this kind of exercise.

And because I ever thought examples to be the best kind of teaching, I will recite a golden sentence out of that poet which is next unto Homer, not only in time but also in worthiness, which hath been a pattern for many worthy wits to follow by this kind of *metaphrasis,* but I will content myself with four workmen, two in Greek and two in Latin, such as in both the tongues wiser and worthier cannot be looked for. Surely no stone set in gold by most cunning workmen is indeed, if right count be made, more worthy the looking on than this golden sentence diversely wrought upon by such four excellent masters.

### Hesiodus. 2

1. Οὗτος μὲν πανάριστος, ὃς αὐτὸς πάντα νοήσῃ
   φρασσάμενος, τά κ' ἔπειτα καὶ ἐς τέλος ᾖσιν ἀμείνω·
2. ἐσθλὸς δ' αὖ κἀκεῖνος, ὃς εὖ εἰπόντι πίθηται·
3. ὃς δέ κε μήτ' αὐτὸς νοέῃ, μήτ' ἄλλου ἀκούων
   ἐν θυμῷ βάλληται, ὃ δ' αὖτ' ἀχρήιος ἀνήρ.[66]

Thus rudely turned into base English:

1. That man in wisdom passeth all,
   to know the best who hath a head:
2. And meetly wise eke counted shall,
   who yields himself to wise men's rede: [67]
3. Who hath no wit, nor none will hear,
   amongst all fools the bell may bear.

[66] *Works and Days,* 293–297.    [67] Counsel.

# The Ready Way to the Latin Tongue

## Sophocles in *Antigone*

1. Φήμ' ἔγωγε, πρεσβεύειν πολὺ
   Φῦναι τὸν ἄνδρα, πάντ' ἐπιστήμης πλέων·
2. εἰ δ' οὖν (φιλεῖ γὰρ τοῦτο μὴ ταύτῃ ῥέπειν)
   καὶ τῶν λεγόντων εὖ καλὸν τὸ μανθάνειν.[68]

Mark the wisdom of Sophocles in leaving out the last sentence because it was not comely for the son to use it to his father.

## Divus Basileus in his "Exhortation to Youth"

Μέμνησθε τοῦ Ἐσιόδου, ὅσ φῆσι, ἄριστον μὲν εἶναι τὸν παρ' ἑαυτοῦ τά δέοντα ξυνορῶντα · ἐσθλὸν δὲ κακεῖνον, τὸν τοῖς παρ' ἑτέρων ὑποδειχθεῖσιν ἐπόμενον· τὸν δὲ πρὸς οὐδέτερον ἐπιτήδειον, ἀρχεῖον εἶναι πρὸς ἄπαντα.[69]

## Marcus Cicero *Pro Aulo Cluentio*

1. *Sapientissimum esse dicunt eum, cui, quod opus sit, ipsi veniat in mentem:* 2. *Proxime accedere illum, qui alterius bene inventis obtemperet.* 3. *In stultitia contra est: minus enim stultus est is, cui nihil in mentem venit, quam ille, qui, quod stulte alteri venit in mentem comprobat.*[70]

---

[68] "I'll say 'tis best of all to be endowed
With absolute wisdom; but, if that's denied,
(And nature takes not readily that ply)
Next wise is he who lists to sage advice" (720–723).
Reprinted by permission of the publishers and the Loeb Classical Library from *Sophocles,* trans. F. Storr, I (Cambridge, Mass.: Harvard University Press, 1962), 369.

[69] "Remember [Hesiod, who said] . . . : 'Best is the man who sees of himself at once what must be done, and excellent is he too who follows what is well indicated by others, but he who is suited for neither is useless in all respects'" (St. Basil, "To Young Men," i.3). Reprinted by permission of the publishers and the Loeb Classical Library from St. Basil, *The Letters,* trans. Roy J. Deferrari, I (Cambridge, Mass.: Harvard University Press, 1950), 381.

[70] "Wisest, they say, is he whose own mind suggests the appropriate idea: next comes the man who accepts the good ideas of another. With

## The Schoolmaster

Cicero doth not plainly express the last sentence, but doth invent it fitly for his purpose: to taunt the folly and simplicity in his adversary, Actius, not weighing wisely the subtle doings of Chrysogonus and Staienus.

### Titus Livius in "Oratione Minutii." Liber 22

1. *Saepe ego audivi milites: eum primum esse virum, qui ipse consulat, quid in rem sit:* 2. *Secundum eum, qui bene monenti obediat:* 3. *Qui, nec ipse consulere, nec alteri parere scit, eum extremi esse ingenii.*[71]

Now which of all these four—Sophocles, St. Basil, Cicero, or Livy—hath expressed Hesiodus best, the judgment is as hard as the workmanship of every one is most excellent indeed. Another example out of the Latin tongue also I will recite for the worthiness of the workman thereof, and that is Horace, who hath so turned the beginning of Terence's *Eunuchus* as doth work in me a pleasant admiration as oft soever as I compare those two places together. And though every master, and every good scholar too, do know the places, both in Terence and Horace, yet I will set them here in one place together that with more pleasure they may be compared together.

### Terentius in *Eunucho*

*Quid igitur faciam? non eam? ne nunc quidem cum accersor ultro? an potius ita me comparem, non perpeti meretricum contumelias?*

---

folly the reverse is true: for he whose mind suggests to him nothing at all is less of a fool than the man who adopts the foolish suggestions of his neighbor" (xxxi.84). Reprinted by permission of the publishers and the Loeb Classical Library from Cicero, *The Speeches*, trans. H. Grose Hodge (Cambridge, Mass.: Harvard University Press, 1961), pp. 311–313.

[71] "Soldiers, I have often heard that the best man is he who can himself advise us what is profitable; the next best he who listens to good advice; but that he who can neither counsel well nor obey another has the meanest capacity of all" (XXII.xxix.8). Reprinted by permission of the publishers and the Loeb Classical Library from *Livy*, trans. B. O. Foster *et al.*, V (Cambridge, Mass.: Harvard University Press, 1963), 299–301.

## The Ready Way to the Latin Tongue

*exclusit: revocat, redeam? non, si me obsecret.* PARMENO (a little after): *Here, quae res in se neque consilium neque modum habet ullum, eam consilio regere non potes. In amore haec omnia insunt vitia, injuriae, suspiciones, inimicitiae, induciae, bellum, pax rursum. Incerta haec si tu postules ratione insanias.*[72]

Horatius *Liber sermonum 2.* Satira 3

*Nec nunc cum me vocet ultro,*
*accedam? an potius mediter finire dolores?*
*exclusit: revocat, redeam? non si obsecret. Ecce*
*servus non paulo sapientior: o here, quae res*
*nec modum habet, neque consilium, ratione modoque*
*tractari non vult. In amore, haec sunt mala, bellum,*
*pax rursum: haec si quis tempestatis prope ritu*
*mobilia, et caeca fluitantia forte, laboret*
*reddere certa, sibi nihilo plus explicet, ac si*
*insanire paret certa ratione, modoque.*[73]

[72] "What am I to do then? Not go even when she invites me herself? Or would it be better to set myself not to put up with the insults of such women? She shut me out, now she recalls me; am I to go back? No, not if she implored me." PARMENO (a little after): "Sir, . . . when a thing lacks method and measure, no method of advice can direct it. Love has in it all these evils: wrongs, jealousies, quarrels, reconcilements, war, then peace again. If you tried to turn these uncertainties into certainties by a system of reasoning, you'd do no more good than if you set yourself to be mad on a system" (I.46–50, 57–63). In early editions, the comedies of Terence were often printed as prose, but Ascham clearly knew that they had been written in verse (see p. 144). Reprinted by permission of the publishers and the Loeb Classical Library from *Terence*, trans. John Sargeaunt, I (Cambridge, Mass.: Harvard University Press, 1959), 241.

[73] " 'Shall I not go even now, when she invites me of her own accord? Or rather, shall I think of putting an end to my affliction? She shut me out. She calls me back. Shall I return? No—not if she implores me.' Now listen to the slave, wiser by far of the two: 'My master, a thing that admits of neither method nor sense cannot be handled by rule and method. In love inhere these evils—first war, then peace: things almost as fickle as the weather, shifting about by blind chance, and if one were to try to reduce them to fixed rule for himself, he would no more set them right than if he aimed at going mad by fixed rule and method' " (262–271). Reprinted by permission of the publishers and the Loeb Classical Library from Horace,

*105*

## The Schoolmaster

This exercise may bring much profit to ripe heads and staid judgments, because in travailing in it the mind must needs be very attentive and busily occupied in turning and tossing itself many ways and conferring with great pleasure the variety of worthy wits and judgments together. But this harm may soon come thereby, and namely to young scholars, lest in seeking other words and new form of sentences they chance upon the worse, for the which only cause Cicero thinketh this exercise not to be fit for young men.

## *Epitome*

This is a way of study belonging rather to matter than to words, to memory than to utterance, to those that be learned already, and hath small place at all amongst young scholars in grammar schools. It may profit privately some learned men, but it hath hurt generally learning itself very much. For by it have we lost whole Trogus, the best part of Titus Livius, the goodly dictionary of Pompeius Festus, a great deal of the civil law,[74] and many other notable books, for the which cause I do the more mislike this exercise, both in old and young.

*Epitome* is good privately for himself that doth work it, but ill commonly for all other that use other men's labor therein: a silly, poor kind of study, not unlike to the doing of those poor folk which neither till, nor sow, nor reap themselves, but glean by stealth upon other men's grounds. Such have empty barns for dear years.

Grammar schools have few *epitomes* to hurt them, except

---

Satires, Epistles, and Ars Poetica, trans. H. Rushton Fairclough (Cambridge, Mass.: Harvard University Press, 1961), p. 175.

[74] Ascham mentions four examples of epitome that have outlived or have been more widely known than their originals: Justin's, of Trogus Pompeius' *Philippic Histories;* Florus', of Livy; Paulus', of Sextus Pompeius Festus' *De verborum significatione;* and, finally, the widely used *Digests* of the whole code of the Roman civil law.

*Epitheta Textoris* [75] and such beggarly gatherings as Horman, Whittinton, and other like vulgars for making of Latins; yea, I do wish that all rules for young scholars were shorter than they be. For without doubt *grammatica* itself is sooner and surer learned by examples of good authors than by the naked rules of grammarians. *Epitome* hurteth more in the universities and study of philosophy, but most of all in divinity itself.

Indeed, books of commonplaces be very necessary to induce a man into an orderly general knowledge, how to refer orderly all that he readeth *ad certa rerum capita* [76] and not wander in study. And to that end did Petrus Lombardus the Master of Sentences and Philip Melanchthon in our days write two notable books of commonplaces.[77]

But to dwell in *epitomes* and books of commonplaces, and not to bind himself daily by orderly study to read with all diligence principally the holiest scripture and withal the best doctors, and so to learn to make true difference betwixt the authority of the one and the counsel of the other, maketh so many seeming and sunburnt ministers as we have, whose learning is gotten in a summer heat and washed away with a Christmas snow again; who nevertheless are less to be blamed than those blind buzzards who in late years, of willful maliciousness, would neither learn themselves nor could teach others anything at all.

*Paraphrasis* hath done less hurt to learning than *epitome*, for

[75] Jean Tixier de Ravisi (Ravisius Textor), *Specimen epithetorum* (Paris, 1518).
[76] To established categories of topics (for example, according to the headings in the Aristotelian system under which all subjects were to be classified).
[77] Petrus Lombardus' *Libri sententiarum* (12th century), the most widely used theological textbook of the Middle Ages; Melanchthon's *Loci communes rerum theologicarum* (Basel, 1521), which Ascham assigned to the Princess Elizabeth while serving as her tutor.

# The Schoolmaster

no *paraphrasis,* though there be many, shall never take away David's Psalter. Erasmus' *paraphrasis,* being never so good, shall never banish the New Testament.[78] And in another school the *paraphrasis* of Brocardus or Sambucus shall never take Aristotle's *Rhetoric* nor Horace's *De arte poetica* out of learned men's hands.[79]

But, as concerning a school *epitome,* he that would have an example of it, let him read Lucian Περὶ κάλλους,[80] which is the very *epitome* of Isocrates' oration *De laudibus Helenae,* whereby he may learn, at the least, this wise lesson: that a man ought to beware to be overbold in altering an excellent man's work.

Nevertheless, some kind of *epitome* may be used by men of skillful judgment to the great profit also of others. As if a wise man would take Hall's Chronicle,[81] where much good matter is quite marred with indenture English,[82] and first change strange and inkhorn[83] terms into proper and commonly used words, next, specially to weed out that that is superfluous and idle, not only where words be vainly heaped one upon another but also where many sentences of one meaning be so clouted up[84] together as though Master Hall had been, not writing the story

[78] Erasmus' paraphrase of nearly the entire New Testament (1517–1524) appeared at London in an English translation in 1548–1549; every parish church in England was ordered to have a copy of it available alongside the Bible.

[79] Jacopo Brocardo, *Partitiones oratoriae, quibus rhetorica Aristotelis praecepta explicantur* (Venice, 1558); Johannes Sambucus, whose paraphrase of and commentary on *De arte poetica* was published at Antwerp in 1564.

[80] The Περὶ κάλλους, or *Charidemus,* is no longer generally considered to be by Lucian.

[81] Edward Hall, *The Union of the Two Noble and Illustre Famelies of Lancastre and York* (London, 1542), popularly known as Hall's Chronicle.

[82] The sort of language used in legal documents.

[83] Bookish, pedantic.     [84] Clumsily arranged.

of England, but varying a sentence in Hitchin [85] school—surely a wise, learned man by this way of *epitome*, in cutting away words and sentences and diminishing nothing at all of the matter, should leave to men's use a story half as much as it was in quantity but twice as good as it was both for pleasure and also commodity.

Another kind of *epitome* may be used likewise very well to much profit. Some man, either by lustiness of nature or brought by ill teaching to a wrong judgment, is overfull of words, sentences, and matter, and yet all his words be proper, apt, and well chosen, all his sentences be round and trimly framed, his whole matter grounded upon good reason and stuffed with full arguments for his intent and purpose. Yet when his talk shall be heard or his writing be read of such one as is either of my two dearest friends, Master Haddon at home or John Sturmius in Germany, that *nimium* in him, which fools and unlearned will most commend, shall either of these two bite his lip or shake his head at it.

This fullness, as it is not to be misliked in a young man, so in farther age, in greater skill, and weightier affairs, it is to be temperated, or else discretion and judgment shall seem to be wanting in him. But if his style be still overrank and lusty, as some men being never so old and spent by years will still be full of youthful conditions (as was Sir Francis Bryan,[86] and evermore would have been), such a rank and full writer must use, if he will do wisely, the exercise of a very good kind of *epitome*, and do as certain wise men do that be overfat and fleshy, who, leaving their own full and plentiful table, go to sojourn abroad from home for a while at the temperate diet of some sober man, and so by little and little cut away the grossness that is in them.

[85] A town in Hertfordshire. The allusion is obscure, since the grammar school of Hitchin was not founded until 1632.

[86] Privy Councilor and favorite of King Henry VIII.

As for an example: if Osorius would leave off his lustiness in striving against St. Austin and his overrank railing against poor Luther and the truth of God's doctrine, and give his whole study not to write anything of his own for a while, but to translate Demosthenes with so strait, fast, and temperate a style in Latin as he is in Greek, he would become so perfect and pure a writer, I believe, as hath been few or none since Cicero's days and so, by doing himself and all learned much good, do others less harm and Christ's doctrine less injury than he doth, and withal win unto himself many worthy friends who, agreeing with him gladly in the love and liking of excellent learning, are sorry to see so worthy a wit, so rare eloquence, wholly spent and consumed in striving with God and good men.

Amongst the rest, no man doth lament him more than I, not only for the excellent learning that I see in him, but also because there hath passed privately betwixt him and me sure tokens of much good will and friendly opinion, the one toward the other. And surely the distance betwixt London and Lisbon should not stop any kind of friendly duty that I could either show to him or do to his, if the greatest matter of all did not in certain points separate our minds.

And yet for my part, both toward him and divers others here at home, for like cause of excellent learning, great wisdom, and gentle humanity which I have seen in them and felt at their hands myself, where the matter of difference is mere conscience in a quiet mind inwardly and not contentious malice with spiteful railing openly, I can be content to follow this rule: in misliking some one thing, not to hate for anything else.

But as for all the bloody beasts, as that fat boar of the wood or those brawling bulls of Bashan,[87] or any lurking dormouse, blind, not by nature but by malice and, as may be gathered of their own testimony, given over to blindness for giving over

[87] "The boar out of the wood" that wastes the vine of the Lord is mentioned in Psalms 80:13, the "strong bulls of Bashan" in Psalms 22:12.

## The Ready Way to the Latin Tongue

God and his word, or such as be so lusty runagates [88] as, first, run from God and his true doctrine, then, from their lords, masters, and all duty, next, from themselves and out of their wits, lastly, from their prince, country, and all due allegiance— whether they ought to be pitied of good men for their misery or contemned of wise men for their malicious folly let good and wise men determine.

And, to return to *epitome* again, some will judge much boldness in me thus to judge of Osorius' style, but wise men do know that mean lookers-on may truly say for a well-made picture, "This face had been more comely if that high red in the cheek were somewhat more pure sanguine than it is," and yet the stander-by cannot amend it himself by any way.

And this is not written to the dispraise but to the great commendation of Osorius, because Tully himself had the same fullness in him and therefore went to Rhodes to cut it away, and saith himself: *Recepi me domum prope mutatus, nam quasi referverat iam oratio.*[89] Which was brought to pass, I believe, not only by the teaching of Molo Apollonius but also by a good way of *epitome* in binding himself to translate *meros Atticos oratores*[90] and so to bring his style from all loose grossness to such firm fastness in Latin as is in Demosthenes in Greek. And this to be most true may easily be gathered, not only of Lucius Crassus' talk in first *De oratore*,[91] but specially of Cicero's own deed in translating Demosthenes' and Aeschines' orations Περὶ στεφάνου to that very end and purpose.[92]

[88] Renegades.

[89] *Brutus,* xci.316. Ascham quotes very inaccurately Cicero's comment on his experience: "Thus I came back after two years' absence not only better trained, but almost transformed . . . my language had lost its froth. . . ." Reprinted by permission of the publishers and the Loeb Classical Library from Cicero, *Brutus,* trans. G. L. Hendrickson (Cambridge, Mass.: Harvard University Press, 1962), p. 275.

[90] The pure Attic orators.     [91] Xxxiv.155.

[92] Mentioned by Cicero in *De optimo genere oratorum,* V.14.

# The Schoolmaster

And although a man groundly learned already may take much profit himself in using by *epitome* to draw other men's works for his own memory's sake into shorter room, as Canterus hath done very well the whole *Metamorphoses* of Ovid, and David Chytraeus a great deal better the nine Muses of Herodotus, and Melanchthon in mine opinion far best of all the whole story of time,[93] not only to his own use, but to other men's profit and his great praise, yet *epitome* is most necessary of all in a man's own writing, as we learn of that noble poet Virgil, who, if Donatus say true, in writing that perfect work of the *Georgics*, used daily when he had written forty or fifty verses not to cease cutting, paring, and polishing of them till he had brought them to the number of ten or twelve.[94]

And this exercise is not more needfully done in a great work than wisely done in your common daily writing, either of letter or other thing else; that is to say, to peruse diligently and see and spy wisely what is always more than needeth. For twenty to one offend more in writing too much than too little, even as twenty to one fall into sickness rather by overmuch fullness than by any lack or emptiness. And therefore is he always the best English physician that best can give a purgation, that is, by way of *epitome,* to cut all overmuch away. And surely men's bodies be not more full of ill humors than commonly men's

[93] Gulielmus Canterus' epitome appears in *P. Ovidii Nasonis Metamorphoseon lib.xv* (Antwerp, 1566); the epitome of Herodotus attributed to David Chytraeus the Elder appears on nine broadsides, dated 1559–1561, bound with the edition of the *Histories* published at Basel, 1557; Melanchthon's epitome of universal history appeared in the Lyons, 1560, edition of Johann Carion, *Chronicon absolutissimum ab orbe condito,* a work first edited by Melanchthon in 1532.

[94] *Vita Virgilii,* IX.33: *Quum Georgica scriberet, traditur quotidie meditatos mane plurimos versus dictare solitus, ac per totum diem retractando ad paucissimas redigere* (P. Virgilius Maro, *Opera omnia,* ed. Chr. Gottl. Heyne, VII [Paris, 1819], 276).

minds (if they be young, lusty, proud, like and love themselves well, as most men do) be full of fancies, opinions, errors, and faults, not only in inward invention but also in all their utterance, either by pen or talk.

And of all other men, even those that have the inventivest heads for all purposes and roundest tongues in all matters and places (except they learn and use this good lesson of *epitome*) commit commonly greater faults than dull, staying-silent men do. For quick inventors and fair, ready speakers, being boldened with their present ability to say more, and perchance better too, at the sudden for that present than any other can do, use less help of diligence and study than they ought to do and so have in them commonly less learning and weaker judgment for all deep considerations than some duller heads and slower tongues have.

And therefore ready speakers generally be not the best, plainest, and wisest writers, nor yet the deepest judgers in weighty affairs, because they do not tarry to weigh and judge all things as they should, but having their heads overfull of matter, be like pens overfull of ink, which will sooner blot than make any fair letter at all. Time was when I had experience of two ambassadors in one place, the one of a hot head to invent and of a hasty hand to write, the other cold and staid in both, but what difference of their doings was made by wise men is not unknown to some persons. The Bishop of Winchester, Stephen Gardiner, had a quick head and a ready tongue and yet was not the best writer in England. Cicero in *Brutus* doth wisely note the same in Sergius Galbo and Quintus Hortensius, who were both hot, lusty, and plain speakers but cold, loose, and rough writers. And Tully telleth the cause why, saying, when they spake their tongue was naturally carried with full tide and wind of their wit; when they wrote their head was solitary, dull, and calm, and so their style was blunt and their writing cold: *Quod vitium* (saith Cicero) *peringeniosis hominibus neque satis doctis plerumque accidit.*[95]

And therefore all quick inventors and ready, fair speakers must be careful that to their goodness of nature they add also in any wise study, labor, leisure, learning, and judgment, and then they shall indeed pass all other, as I know some do, in whom all those qualities are fully planted; or else, if they give overmuch to their wit and overlittle to their labor and learning, they will soonest overreach in talk and farthest come behind in writing whatsoever they take in hand. The method of *epitome* is most necessary for such kind of men. And thus much concerning the use or misuse of all kind of *epitomes* in matters of learning.

## Imitatio

Imitation is a faculty to express lively and perfectly that example which ye go about to follow. And of itself it is large and wide, for all the works of nature in a manner be examples for art to follow.

But to our purpose. All languages, both learned and mother tongues, be gotten, and gotten only, by imitation. For as ye use to hear, so ye learn to speak; if ye hear no other, ye speak not yourself, and whom ye only hear, of them ye only learn.

And therefore if ye would speak as the best and wisest do, ye must be conversant where the best and wisest are, but if you be born or brought up in a rude country, ye shall not choose but speak rudely. The rudest man of all knoweth this to be true.

Yet nevertheless the rudeness of common and mother tongues is no bar for wise speaking. For in the rudest country and most barbarous mother language many be found can speak very wisely, but in the Greek and Latin tongue, the two only learned tongues which be kept not in common talk but in private books, we find always wisdom and eloquence, good matter and good

[95] Slightly misquoted from *Brutus,* xxiv.92: "the case frequently with men of unusual talent but insufficient training. . . ."

utterance, never or seldom asunder. For all such authors as be fullest of good matter and right judgment in doctrine be likewise always most proper in words, most apt in sentence, most plain and pure in uttering the same.

And contrariwise, in those two tongues all writers, either in religion or any sect of philosophy, whosoever be found fond in judgment of matter, be commonly found as rude in uttering their mind. For Stoics, Anabaptists, and friars, with Epicures, libertines, and monks, being most like in learning and life, are no fonder and pernicious in their opinions than they be rude and barbarous in their writings. They be not wise, therefore, that say, "What care I for a man's words and utterance if his matter and reasons be good?" Such men say so, not so much of ignorance as either of some singular pride in themselves, or some special malice of other, or for some private and partial matter, either in religion or other kind of learning. For good and choice meats be no more requisite for healthy bodies than proper and apt words be for good matters and also plain and sensible utterance for the best and deepest reasons, in which two points standeth perfect eloquence, one of the fairest and rarest gifts that God doth give to man.

Ye know not what hurt ye do to learning that care not for words but for matter and so make a divorce betwixt the tongue and the heart. For mark all ages, look upon the whole course of both the Greek and Latin tongue, and ye shall surely find that when apt and good words began to be neglected and properties of those two tongues to be confounded, then also began ill deeds to spring, strange manners to oppress good orders, new and fond opinions to strive with old and true doctrine, first in philosophy and after in religion, right judgment of all things to be perverted, and so virtue with learning is contemned and study left off. Of ill thoughts cometh perverse judgment; of ill deeds springeth lewd talk. Which four misorders, as they mar man's life, so destroy they good learning withal.

But behold the goodness of God's providence for learning: all old authors and sects of philosophy which were fondest in opinion and rudest in utterance, as Stoics and Epicures, first contemned of wise men and after forgotten of all men, be so consumed by times as they be now not only out of use but also out of memory of man; which thing, I surely think, will shortly chance to the whole doctrine and all the books of fantastical Anabaptists and friars, and of the beastly libertines and monks.

Again behold on the other side how God's wisdom hath wrought, that of *Academici* and *Peripatetici,* those that were wisest in judgment of matters and purest in uttering their minds, the first and chiefest that wrote most and best in either tongue, as Plato and Aristotle in Greek, Tully in Latin, be so either wholly or sufficiently left unto us as I never knew yet scholar that gave himself to like, and love, and follow chiefly those three authors but he proved both learned, wise, and also an honest man, if he joined withal the true doctrine of God's holy Bible, without the which the other three be but fine-edged tools in a fool's or madman's hand.

But to return to imitation again, there be three kinds of it in matters of learning.

The whole doctrine of comedies and tragedies is a perfect imitation or fair, lively painted picture of the life of every degree of man. Of this imitation writeth Plato at large in third *De republica,*[96] but it doth not much belong at this time to our purpose.

The second kind of imitation is to follow for learning of tongues and sciences the best authors. Here riseth amongst proud and envious wits a great controversy whether one or many are to be followed, and if one, who is that one—Seneca or Cicero, Sallust or Caesar, and so forth in Greek and Latin.

The third kind of imitation belongeth to the second, as when you be determined whether ye will follow one or more, to know

[96] 394B–398B.

perfectly and which way to follow that one; in what place, by what mean and order, by what tools and instruments ye shall do it; by what skill and judgment ye shall truly discern whether ye follow rightly or no.

This *imitatio* is *dissimilis materei similis tractatio* and also *similis materei dissimilis tractatio*,[97] as Virgil followed Homer, but the argument to the one was Ulysses, to the other Aeneas. Tully persecuted Antony with the same weapons of eloquence that Demosthenes used before against Philip.

Horace followeth Pindar, but either of them his own argument and person, as the one, Hiero, King of Sicily, the other, Augustus the Emperor, and yet both for like respects, that is, for their courageous stoutness in war and just government in peace.

One of the best examples for right imitation we lack, and that is Menander, whom our Terence (as the matter required) in like argument, in the same persons, with equal eloquence, foot by foot did follow.

Some pieces remain, like broken jewels, whereby men may rightly esteem and justly lament the loss of the whole.

Erasmus, the ornament of learning in our time, doth wish that some man of learning and diligence would take the like pains in Demosthenes and Tully that Macrobius hath done in Homer and Virgil, that is, to write out and join together where the one doth imitate the other.[98] Erasmus' wish is good, but surely it is not good enough; for Macrobius' gatherings for the *Aeneidos* out of Homer, and Eobanus Hessus' more diligent gatherings for the *Bucolics* out of Theocritus,[99] as they be not fully taken

[97] Similar treatment of dissimilar matter and also dissimilar treatment of similar matter.

[98] *Epistolae* (Leyden, 1706), col. 1448A–B. See also Erasmus' preface to Δημοσθένους λόγοι δυὸ καὶ εξήκοντα (Basel, 1532), sig. a2v.

[99] Macrobius, *Saturnalia,* III.ii–xvi. The frequently reprinted comments on Virgil's *Eclogues* by Helius Eobanus Hessus, translator of Theocritus, were published at Haguenau in 1529.

out of the whole heap as they should be, but even as though they had not sought for them of purpose but found them scattered here and there by chance in their way, even so, only to point out and nakedly to join together their sentences, with no farther declaring the manner and way how the one doth follow the other, were but a cold help to the increase of learning.

But if a man would take this pain also, when he hath laid two places of Homer and Virgil or of Demosthenes and Tully together, to teach plainly withal after this sort:

1. Tully retaineth thus much of the matter, these sentences, these words.

2. This and that he leaveth out, which he doth wittily to this end and purpose.

3. This he addeth here.

4. This he diminisheth there.

5. This he ordereth thus, with placing that here, not there.

6. This he altereth and changeth either in property of words, in form of sentence, in substance of the matter, or in one or other convenient circumstance of the author's present purpose. In these few rude English words are wrapped up all the necessary tools and instruments wherewith true imitation is rightly wrought withal in any tongue. Which tools, I openly confess, be not of mine own forging but partly left unto me by the cunningest master and one of the worthiest gentlemen that ever England bred, Sir John Cheke, partly borrowed by me out of the shop of the dearest friend I have out of England, Joannes Sturmius. And therefore I am the bolder to borrow of him and here to leave them to other, and namely to my children; which tools, if it please God that another day they may be able to use rightly, as I do wish and daily pray they may do, I shall be more glad than if I were able to leave them a great quantity of land.

This foresaid order and doctrine of imitation would bring forth more learning and breed up truer judgment than any other exercise that can be used, but not for young beginners, because they shall not be able to consider duly thereof. And truly it may be a shame to good students who, having so fair examples to follow as Plato and Tully, do not use so wise ways in following them for the obtaining of wisdom and learning as rude, ignorant artificers do for gaining a small commodity. For surely the meanest painter useth more wit, better art, greater diligence in his shop in following the picture of any mean man's face than commonly the best students do, even in the university, for the attaining of learning itself.

Some ignorant, unlearned, and idle student, or some busy looker upon this little poor book that hath neither will to do good himself nor skill to judge right of others, but can lustily contemn by pride and ignorance all painful diligence and right order in study, will perchance say that I am too precise, too curious,[100] in marking and piddling thus about the imitation of others, and that the old worthy authors did never busy their heads and wits in following so precisely either the matter what other men wrote or else the manner how other men wrote. They will say it were a plain slavery, and injury too, to shackle and tie a good wit and hinder the course of a man's good nature with such bonds of servitude in following other.

Except such men think themselves wiser than Cicero for teaching of eloquence, they must be content to turn a new leaf.

The best book that ever Tully wrote, by all men's judgment and by his own testimony too, in writing whereof he employed most care, study, learning, and judgment, is his book *De oratore ad Quintum fratrem.* Now let us see what he did for the matter and also for the manner of writing thereof. For the whole book consisteth in these two points only: in good matter and good handling of the matter. And first for the matter, it is whole Aristotle's, whatsoever Antony in the second and Crassus in the third doth teach. Trust not me, but believe Tully himself, who writeth so, first in that goodly long epistle *Ad Publium Lentu-*

[100] Fastidious.

*lum*, and after in divers places *Ad Atticum*.[101] And in the very
book itself Tully will not have it hidden, but both Catulus and
Crassus do oft and pleasantly lay that stealth to Antonius'
charge. Now for the handling of the matter, was Tully so
precise and curious rather to follow another man's pattern than
to invent some new shape himself, namely in that book wherein
he purposed to leave to posterity the glory of his wit? Yea,
forsooth, that he did. And this is not my guessing and gathering, nor only performed by Tully in very deed, but uttered also
by Tully in plain words to teach other men thereby what they
should do in taking like matter in hand.

And that which is specially to be marked, Tully doth utter
plainly his conceit and purpose therein by the mouth of the
wisest man in all that company, for saith Scaevola himself: *Cur
non imitamur, Crasse, Socratem illum, qui est in Phaedro Platonis, etc?* [102]

And further to understand that Tully did not *obiter* and by
chance, but purposely and mindfully bend himself to a precise
and curious imitation of Plato concerning the shape and form of
those books, mark, I pray you, how curious Tully is to utter his
purpose and doing therein, writing thus to Atticus:

*Quod in his Oratoriis libris, quos tantopere laudas, personam desid-
eras Scaevolae, non eam temere dimovi: sed feci idem, quod in
πολιτεία deus ille noster Plato, cum in Piraeum Socrates venisset
ad Cephalum locupletem et festivum senem, quoad primus ille
sermo haberetur, adest in disputando senex, deinde, cum ipse
quoque commodissime locutus esset, ad rem divinam dicit se velle
discedere, neque postea revertitur. Credo Platonem vix putasse
satis consonum fore, si hominem id aetatis in tam longo sermone
diutius retinuisset. Multo ego satius hoc mihi cavendum putavi in
Scaevola, qui et aetate et valetudine erat ea qua meministi, et his*

[101] *Familiares*, I.ix.23; *Epistolae ad Atticum*, IV.xvi.
[102] *De oratore*, I.vii.28: "Crassus, why do we not imitate Socrates as he
appears in the *Phaedrus* of Plato?"

*honoribus, ut vix satis decorum videretur eum plures dies esse in Crassi Tusculano. Et erat primi libri sermo non alienus a Scaevolae studiis, reliqui libri* τεκνολογίαν *habent, ut scis. Huic joculatoriae disputationi senem illum, ut noras, interesse sane nolui.*[103]

If Cicero had not opened himself and declared his own thought and doings herein, men that be idle, and ignorant, and envious of other men's diligence and well-doings would have sworn that Tully had never minded any such thing, but that of a precise curiosity we feign and forge and father such things of Tully as he never meant indeed. I write this not for nought, for I have heard some both well learned and other ways very wise that by their lusty misliking of such diligence have drawn back the forwardness of very good wits. But even as such men themselves do sometimes stumble upon doing well by chance and benefit of good wit, so would I have our scholar always able to do well by order of learning and right skill of judgment.

Concerning imitation many learned men have written, with

[103] *Ad Atticum,* IV.xvi: "While praising those books, you miss the character of Scaevola from the scene. It was not without good reason that I removed him. Our god Plato did the same in his *Republic.* When Socrates called on that wealthy and cheery old soul Cephalus in the Piraeus, the old man takes part in the discussion during the introductory conversation; but after a very neat speech, he pleads that he wants to go to a divine service, and does not come back again. I fancy Plato thought it would have been inartistic to keep a man of that age any longer in so lengthy a discussion. I thought there was still more reason to be careful in the case of Scaevola, who was at the age and in the state of health in which you must remember he was, and was crowned with such honors that it would hardly have been proper for him to spend several days with Crassus at his villa at Tusculum. Besides, the talk in the first book was not unconnected with Scaevola's pursuits: while the remaining books contained a technical discussion, as you know. In such I did not like the merry old man, you remember, to take a part." Reprinted by permission of the publishers and the Loeb Classical Library from Cicero, *Letters to Atticus,* trans. E. O. Winstedt, I (Cambridge, Mass.: Harvard University Press, 1956), 315.

much diversity for the matter and therefore with great contrariety and some stomach [104] amongst themselves. I have read as many as I could get diligently, and what I think of every one of them I will freely say my mind. With which freedom I trust good men will bear because it shall tend to neither spiteful nor harmful controversy.

In Tully it is well touched, shortly taught, not fully declared by Antonius in second *De oratore*, and afterward in *Orator ad Brutum*, for the liking and misliking of Isocrates, and the contrary judgment of Tully against Calvus, Brutus, and Calidius, *de genere dicendi Attico et Asiatico*.[105]

Dionysius Halicarnasseus' Περὶ μιμήσεως I fear is lost; which author, next Aristotle, Plato, and Tully, of all other that write of eloquence, by the judgment of them that be best learned, deserveth the next praise and place.

Quintilian writeth of it shortly and coldly for the matter, yet hotly and spitefully enough against the imitation of Tully.[106]

Erasmus, being more occupied in spying other men's faults than declaring his own advice, is mistaken of many, to the great hurt of study, for his authority's sake. For he writeth rightly, rightly understanded, he and Longolius only differing in this: that the one seemeth to give overmuch, the other overlittle, to him whom they both best loved and chiefly allowed of all other.[107]

Budaeus in his *Commentaries* roughly and obscurely after his

[104] Spite.

[105] *De oratore*, II.xxi.89–xxiii.98; *Orator*, xii.40–42, li.172–lii.176; Cicero's objections to the excessive "Atticism" of Calvus appear in *Brutus*, xvii.67–xviii.69, lxxxii.283–285; of Brutus, in *Orator*, xii.40, lxxi.237; of Calidius, in *Brutus*, lxxix.273–lxxx.278.

[106] *Institutio oratoria*, X.ii.24–26. Ascham is by no means fair here to Quintilian, who recommends imitating Cicero but argues that one should also turn at times to other models.

[107] Erasmus' *Ciceronianus* (Paris, 1528) includes criticism of the efforts made by the Belgian humanist Longolius (Christophe de Longueil) to achieve a strictly Ciceronian style.

kind of writing, and for the matter carried somewhat out of the way in overmuch misliking the imitation of Tully.[108]

Philip Melanchthon, learnedly and truly.[109]

Camerarius, largely, with a learned judgment, but somewhat confusedly and with overrough a style.[110]

Sambucus, largely, with a right judgment, but somewhat a crooked style.[111]

Other have written also, as Cortesius to Politian, and that very well, Bembus *Ad Picum* a great deal better,[112] but Joannes Sturmius *De nobilitate literata* and *De amissa dicendi ratione* far best of all, in mine opinion, that ever took this matter in hand.[113] For all the rest declare chiefly this point: whether one, or many, or all are to be followed; but Sturmius only hath most learnedly declared who is to be followed, what is to be followed, and (the best point of all) by what way and order true imitation is rightly to be exercised. And although Sturmius herein doth far pass all other, yet hath he not so fully and perfectly done it as I do wish he had and as I know he could. For though he hath done it perfectly for precept, yet hath he not done it perfectly enough for example; which he did, neither for lack of skill nor by negligence but of purpose, contented with one or two examples because he was minded in those two books to write of it both shortly and also had to touch other matters.

[108] Budé, *Commentarii linguae Graecae*, pp. 874–875.

[109] "De imitatione," *Elementorum rhetorices libri duo* (Wittenberg, 1539), sigs. Lr–M5v.

[110] Joachim Camerarius, *Elementa rhetoricae* (Basel, 1551), pp. 273–304.

[111] Joannes Sambucus, *De imitatione a Cicerone petenda libri III* (Padua, 1559).

[112] Two of the most famous exchanges over the question whether or not to imitate Cicero alone were those of Paolo Cortesi with Agnolo Poliziano and of Pietro Bembo with Gianfrancesco Pico (see Izora Scott, *Controversies over the Imitation of Cicero* [New York, 1910], *passim*).

[113] *Nobilitas literata ad Werteros fratres* (Strasbourg, 1549); *De amissa dicendi ratione* (Strasbourg, 1538; enlarged edition, 1543).

The Schoolmaster

Bartholomaeus Riccius Ferrariensis also hath written learnedly, diligently, and very largely of this matter [114] even as he did before very well *De apparatu linguae latinae*. He writeth the better, in mine opinion, because his whole doctrine, judgment, and order seemeth to be borrowed out of Joannes Sturmius' books. He addeth also examples, the best kind of teaching, wherein he doth well, but not well enough; indeed, he committeth no fault, but yet deserveth small praise. He is content with the mean and followeth not the best, as a man that would feed upon acorns when he may eat as good cheap [115] the finest wheat bread. He teacheth, for example, where and how two or three late Italian poets do follow Virgil and how Virgil himself in the story of Dido doth wholly imitate Catullus in the like matter of Ariadne; wherein I like better his diligence and order of teaching than his judgment in choice of examples for imitation. But if he had done thus: if he had declared where and how, how oft and how many ways Virgil doth follow Homer, as for example the coming of Ulysses to Alcinous and Calypso with the coming of Aeneas to Carthage and Dido; likewise the games—running, wrestling, and shooting—that Achilles maketh in Homer with the selfsame games that Aeneas maketh in Virgil; the harness of Achilles with the harness of Aeneas, and the manner of making them both by Vulcan; the notable combat betwixt Achilles and Hector with as notable a combat betwixt Aeneas and Turnus; the going down to hell of Ulysses in Homer with the going down to hell of Aeneas in Virgil; and other places infinite more, as similitudes, narrations, messages, descriptions of persons, places, battles, tempests, shipwrecks, and commonplaces for divers purposes, which be as precisely taken out of Homer as ever did painter in London follow the picture of any fair personage. And when these places had been gathered together by this way of diligence, then to

[114] Bartolomeo Ricci, *De imitatione libri tres* (Venice, 1545).
[115] For an equally low price.

124

have conferred them together by this order of teaching: as, diligently to mark what is kept and used in either author in words, in sentences, in matter; what is added; what is left out; what ordered otherwise, either *praeponendo, interponendo,* or *postponendo,* [116] and what is altered for any respect, in word, phrase, sentence, figure, reason, argument, or by any way of circumstance. If Riccius had done this, he had not only been well liked for his diligence in teaching but also justly commended for his right judgment in right choice of examples for the best imitation.

Riccius also for imitation of prose declareth where and how Longolius doth follow Tully, but as for Longolius, I would not have him the pattern of our imitation. Indeed, in Longolius' shop be proper and fair-showing colors, but as for shape, figure, and natural comeliness, by the judgment of best-judging artificers he is rather allowed as one to be borne withal than specially commended as one chiefly to be followed.

If Riccius had taken for his examples where Tully himself followeth either Plato or Demosthenes, he had shot then at the right mark. But to excuse Riccius somewhat, though I cannot fully defend him, it may be said his purpose was to teach only the Latin tongue, when this way that I do wish, to join Virgil with Homer, to read Tully with Demosthenes and Plato, requireth a cunning and perfect master in both the tongues. It is my wish indeed, and that by good reason, for whosoever will write well of any matter must labor to express that that is perfect and not to stay and content himself with the mean. Yea, I say farther, though it be not unpossible, yet it is very rare and marvelous hard to prove excellent in the Latin tongue for him that is not also well seen in the Greek tongue. Tully himself, most excellent of nature, most diligent in labor, brought up from his cradle in that place and in that time where and when

[116] By placing before, between, or after.

the Latin tongue most flourished naturally in every man's mouth, yet was not his own tongue able itself to make him so cunning in his own tongue as he was indeed, but the knowledge and imitation of the Greek tongue withal.

This he confesseth himself, this he uttereth in many places, as those can tell best that use to read him most.

Therefore thou that shootest at perfection in the Latin tongue, think not thyself wiser than Tully was in choice of the way that leadeth rightly to the same; think not thy wit better than Tully's was, as though that may serve thee that was not sufficient for him. For even as a hawk flieth not high with one wing, even so a man reacheth not to excellency with one tongue.

I have been a looker-on in the cockpit of learning these many years, and one cock only have I known which with one wing, even at this day, doth pass all other, in mine opinion, that ever I saw in any pit in England, though they had two wings.[117] Yet nevertheless, to fly well with one wing, to run fast with one leg, be rather rare masteries much to be marveled at than sure examples safely to be followed. A bishop that now liveth, a good man, whose judgment in religion I better like than his opinion in perfectness in other learning, said once unto me, "We have no need now of the Greek tongue when all things be translated into Latin." But the good man understood not that even the best translation is, for mere necessity, but an evil-imped [118] wing to fly withal or a heavy stump leg of wood to go withal; such, the higher they fly, the sooner they falter and fail; the faster they run, the ofter they stumble and sorer they fall. Such as will needs so fly may fly at a pie and catch a daw, and such runners, as commonly they shove and shoulder to stand foremost, yet in the end they come behind others and deserve

---

[117] Almost certainly Walter Haddon, who, though deficient in Greek, was considered at the time the best Latin stylist in England.

[118] Grafted with additional feathers to increase strength.

## The Ready Way to the Latin Tongue

but the hopshackles,[119] if the masters of the game be right judgers.

Therefore in perusing thus so many divers books for imitation, it came into my head that a very profitable book might be made *De imitatione* after another sort than ever yet was attempted of that matter, containing a certain few fit precepts unto the which should be gathered and applied plenty of examples out of the choicest authors of both the tongues. This work would stand rather in good diligence for the gathering and right judgment for the applying of those examples than any great learning or utterance at all.

The doing thereof would be more pleasant than painful, and would bring also much profit to all that should read it and great praise to him would take in it hand, with just desert of thanks.

Erasmus, giving himself to read over all authors Greek and Latin, seemeth to have prescribed to himself this order of reading; that is, to note out by the way three special points: all adages, all similitudes, and all witty sayings of most notable personages. And so by one labor he left to posterity three notable books, and namely two his *Chiliades, Apothegmata,* and *Similiae.*[120] Likewise, if a good student would bend himself to read diligently over Tully, and with him also at the same time as diligently Plato and Xenophon with his books of philosophy, Isocrates and Demosthenes with his orations, and Aristotle with his rhetorics, which five of all other be those whom Tully best loved and specially followed, and would mark diligently in Tully where he doth *exprimere* or *effingere* (which be the very proper words of imitation) either *copiam Platonis* or

---

[119] Hobbles.

[120] That is, the *Adagia*, first published at Venice, 1508, and eventually containing over four thousands (*chiliades*) of proverbs; the *Apothegmata* (Lyons, 1531), or fine sayings of famous men; and a book of comparisons, or *Similiae* (Strasbourg, 1514).

*venustatem Xenophontis, suavitatem Isocratis,* or *vim Demosthenis, propriam et puram subtilitatem Aristotelis,*[121] and not only write out the places diligently and lay them together orderly, but also to confer them with skillful judgment by those few rules which I have expressed now twice before—if that diligence were taken, if that order were used, what perfect knowledge of both the tongues, what ready and pithy utterance in all matters, what right and deep judgment in all kind of learning would follow, is scarcely credible to be believed.

These books be not many, nor long, nor rude in speech, nor mean in matter, but next the majesty of God's holy word most worthy for a man, the lover of learning and honesty, to spend his life in. Yea, I have heard worthy Master Cheke many times say, "I would have a good student pass and journey through all authors both Greek and Latin, but he that will dwell in these few books only, first in God's holy Bible, and then join with it Tully in Latin, Plato, Aristotle, Xenophon, Isocrates, and Demosthenes in Greek, must needs prove an excellent man."

Some men already in our days have put to their helping hands to this work of imitation, as Perionus, Henricus Stephanus in *Dictionario Ciceroniano,* and Petrus Victorius most praiseworthily of all in that his learned work containing twenty-five books *De varia lectione,* in which books be joined diligently together the best authors of both the tongues where one doth seem to imitate another.[122]

But all these, with Macrobius, Hessus, and other, be no more but common porters, carriers, and bringers of matter and stuff together. They order nothing; they lay before you what is done;

---

[121] The fullness of expression of Plato or the grace of Xenophon, the pleasantness of Isocrates or the vigor of Demosthenes, the characteristic and pure plainness of Aristotle.

[122] Joachim Perion, *Ex Platonis Timaeo particula, Ciceronis de universitate libro respondens* (Paris, 1540); Henri Estienne, *Ciceronianum lexicon Graeco-Latinum* (Paris, 1557); Pietro Vettori, *Variarum lectionum libri XXV* (Lyons, 1554).

they do not teach you how it is done; they busy not themselves with form of building; they do not declare, "This stuff is thus framed by Demosthenes, and thus and thus by Tully, and so likewise in Xenophon, Plato, and Isocrates, and Aristotle." For joining Virgil with Homer I have sufficiently declared before.

The like diligence I would wish to be taken in Pindar and Horace, an equal match for all respects.

In tragedies (the goodliest argument of all, and for the use either of a learned preacher or a civil gentleman more profitable than Homer, Pindar, Virgil, and Horace, yea, comparable, in mine opinion, with the doctrine of Aristotle, Plato, and Xenophon) the Grecians Sophocles and Euripides far overmatch our Seneca in Latin, namely in οἰκονομίᾳ *et decoro*, [123] although Seneca's elocution and verse be very commendable for his time. And for the matters of Hercules, Thebes, Hippolytus, and Troy, his imitation is to be gathered into the same book and to be tried by the same touchstone as is spoken before.

In histories, and namely in Livy, the like diligence of imitation could bring excellent learning and breed staid judgment in taking any like matter in hand.

Only Livy were a sufficient task for one man's study, to compare him, first, with his fellow for all respects, Dionysius Halicarnasseus, who both lived in one time, took both one history in hand to write, deserved both like praise of learning and eloquence. Then with Polybius, that wise writer whom Livy professeth to follow, and if he would deny it, yet it is plain that the best part of the third decade in Livy is in a manner translated out of the third and rest of Polybius. Lastly, with Thucydides, to whose imitation Livy is curiously bent, as may well appear by that one oration of those of Campania asking aid of the Romans against the Samnites, which is wholly taken, sentence, reason, argument, and order, out of the oration of

[123] Arrangement and fitness.

Corcyra asking like aid of the *Athenienses* against them of Corinth.[124] If some diligent student would take pains to compare them together, he should easily perceive that I do say true. A book thus wholly filled with examples of imitation, first out of Tully compared with Plato, Xenophon, Isocrates, Demosthenes, and Aristotle, then out of Virgil and Horace with Homer and Pindar, next out of Seneca with Sophocles and Euripides, lastly out of Livy with Thucydides, Polybius, and Halicarnasseus, gathered with good diligence and compared with right order, as I have expressed before, were another manner of work for all kind of learning, and namely for eloquence, than be those cold gatherings of Macrobius, Hessus, Perionus, Stephanus, and Victorius, which may be used, as I said before in this case, as porters and carriers, deserving like praise as such men do wages, but only Sturmius is he out of whom the true survey and whole workmanship is specially to be learned.

I trust this my writing shall give some good student occasion to take some piece in hand of this work of imitation. And as I had rather have any do it than myself, yet surely myself rather than none at all. And by God's grace, if God do lend me life, with health, free leisure and liberty, with good liking and a merry heart I will turn the best part of my study and time to toil in one or other piece of this work of imitation.

This diligence to gather examples to give light and understanding to good precepts is no new invention but specially used of the best authors and oldest writers. For Aristotle himself (as Diogenes Laertius declareth), when he had written that goodly book of the *Topics*, did gather out of stories and orators so many examples as filled fifteen books, only to express the rules of his *Topics*.[125] These were the commentaries that

[124] *Decade* I, Book VII.xxx, imitated from Thucydides, I.xxxii–xxxvi (cited incorrectly in marginal note as Thucydides, X).

[125] I have been unable to locate such an assertion in Diogenes Laertius' biographical sketch of Aristotle; Diogenes speaks only of "a number of

# The Ready Way to the Latin Tongue

Aristotle thought fit for his *Topics,* and therefore, to speak as I think, I never saw yet any commentary upon Aristotle's logic, either in Greek or Latin, that ever I liked, because they be rather spent in declaring schoolpoint rules than in gathering fit examples for use and utterance either by pen or talk. For precepts in all authors, and namely in Aristotle, without applying unto them the imitation of examples, be hard, dry, and cold, and therefore barren, unfruitful, and unpleasant. But Aristotle, namely in his *Topics* and *Elenches,* should be not only fruitful but also pleasant too, if examples out of Plato and other good authors were diligently gathered and aptly applied unto his most perfect precepts there. And it is notable, that my friend Sturmius writeth herein, that there is no precept in Aristotle's *Topics* whereof plenty of examples be not manifest in Plato's works. And I hear say that an excellent learned man, Tomitanus in Italy, hath expressed every fallation [126] in Aristotle with divers examples out of Plato.[127] Would to God I might once see some worthy student of Aristotle and Plato in Cambridge that would join in one book the precepts of the one with the examples of the other. For such a labor were one special piece of that work of imitation which I do wish were gathered together in one volume.

Cambridge, at my first coming thither, but not at my going away, committed this fault in reading the precepts of Aristotle without the examples of other authors. But herein in my time these men of worthy memory—Master Redman, Master Cheke, Master Smith, Master Haddon, Master Watson—put so to their helping hands as that university and all students there, as long

---

propositions, by means of which the student can be furnished with probable arguments for the solving of problems" ( *Lives of Eminent Philosophers,* V.xxix).

[126] Example of a flaw in formal reasoning.

[127] Bernardino Tomitano ( 1517–1576), Italian humanist and professor of logic at Padua, author of *Introductiones ad Sophisticos elenchos . . . Aristotelis* ( Venice, 1544).

as learning shall last, shall be bound unto them, if that trade in study be truly followed which those men left behind them there.

By this small mention of Cambridge I am carried into three imaginations: first, into a sweet remembrance of my time spent there; then, into some careful thoughts for the grievous alteration that followed soon after; lastly, into much joy to hear tell of the good recovery and earnest forwardness in all good learning there again.

To utter these my thoughts somewhat more largely were somewhat beside my matter, yet not very far out of the way, because it shall wholly tend to the good encouragement and right consideration of learning, which is my full purpose in writing this little book; whereby also shall well appear this sentence to be most true, that only good men, by their government and example, make happy times in every degree and state.

Doctor Nicholas Metcalfe, that honorable father, was Master of St. John's College when I came thither—a man meanly learned himself, but not meanly affectioned to set forward learning in others. He found that college spending scarce two hundred marks by year; he left it spending a thousand marks and more. Which he procured, not with his money but by his wisdom; not chargeably bought by him, but liberally given by others by his mean for the zeal and honor they bare to learning. And that which is worthy of memory, all these givers were (almost) northern men who, being liberally rewarded in the service of their prince, bestowed it as liberally for the good of their country. Some men thought, therefore, that Doctor Metcalfe was partial to northern men, but sure I am of this, that northern men were partial in doing more good and giving more lands to the furtherance of learning than any other countrymen in those days did; which deed should have been rather an example of goodness for other to follow than matter of malice

## The Ready Way to the Latin Tongue

for any to envy, as some there were that did. Truly, Doctor Metcalfe was partial to none, but indifferent to all, a master for the whole, a father to everyone in that college. There was none so poor, if he had either will to goodness or wit to learning, that could lack being there or should depart from thence for any need. I am witness myself that money many times was brought into young men's studies by strangers whom they knew not. In which doing this worthy Nicholas followed the steps of good old St. Nicholas, that learned bishop. He was a papist indeed, but would to God amongst all us Protestants I might once see but one that would win like praise in doing like good for the advancement of learning and virtue. And yet, though he were a papist, if any young man given to new learning (as they termed it) went beyond his fellows in wit, labor, and towardness, even the same neither lacked open praise to encourage him nor private exhibition [128] to maintain him, as worthy Sir John Cheke, if he were alive, would bear good witness, and so can many more. I myself, one of the meanest of a great number in that college, because there appeared in me some small show of towardness and diligence, lacked not his favor to further me in learning.

And being a boy, new bachelor of art, I chanced amongst my companions to speak against the Pope, which matter was then in every man's mouth because Doctor Heynes and Doctor Skip [129] were come from the court to debate the same matter by preaching and disputation in the university. This happened the same time when I stood to be fellow there; my talk came to Doctor Metcalfe's ear; I was called before him and the seniors, and after grievous rebuke and some punishment, open warning was given to all the fellows none to be so hardy to give me his voice at that election. And yet for all those open threats the

[128] Financial aid.
[129] Simon Heynes, Vice-Chancellor of the University, and John Skip, later Bishop of Hereford.

good father himself privily procured that I should even then be chosen fellow. But, the election being done, he made countenance of great discontentation thereat. This good man's goodness and fatherly discretion used toward me that one day shall never out of my remembrance all the days of my life. And for the same cause have I put it here in this small record of learning. For next God's providence, surely that day was by that good father's means *dies natalis* [130] to me for the whole foundation of the poor learning I have and of all the furtherance that hitherto elsewhere I have obtained.

This his goodness stood not still in one or two but flowed abundantly over all that college, and brake out also to nourish good wits in every part of that university; whereby, at his departing thence, he left such a company of fellows and scholars in St. John's College as can scarce be found now in some whole university, which, either for divinity on the one side or other, or for civil service to their prince and country, have been and are yet to this day notable ornaments to this whole realm. Yea, St. John's did then so flourish as Trinity College, that princely house now, at the first erection was but *colonia deducta* [131] out of St. John's, not only for their master, fellows, and scholars but also, which is more, for their whole both order of learning and discipline of manners; and yet to this day it never took master but such as was bred up before in St. John's, doing the duty of a good *colonia* to her *metropolis,* as the ancient cities in Greece and some yet in Italy at this day are accustomed to do.

St. John's stood in this state until those heavy times and that grievous change that chanced *anno* 1553 when more perfect scholars were dispersed from thence in one month than many years can rear up again. For when *aper de sylva* [132] had passed the seas and fastened his foot again in England, not only the

[130] A day of birth.    [131] A colony led forth.
[132] The boar out of the wood (see note 87).

two fair groves of learning in England were either cut up by the root or trodden down to the ground and wholly went to wrack, but the young spring [133] there, and everywhere else, was pitifully nipped and overtrodden by very beasts, and also the fairest standers of all were rooted up and cast into the fire, to the great weakening even at this day of Christ's church in England, both for religion and learning.

And what good could chance then to the universities when some of the greatest, though not of the wisest nor best learned nor best men neither of that side, did labor to persuade that ignorance was better than knowledge, which they meant not for the laity only but also for the greatest rabble of their spiritualty,[134] what other pretense openly soever they made; and therefore did some of them at Cambridge (whom I will not name openly) cause hedge priests [135] fetched out of the country to be made fellows in the university, saying in their talk privily and declaring by their deeds openly that he was fellow good enough for their time if he could wear a gown and tippet [136] comely, and have his crown shorn fair and roundly, and could turn his portess and pie [137] readily; which I speak not to reprove any order either of apparel or other duty that may be well and indifferently used, but to note the misery of that time when the benefits provided for learning were so foully misused. And what was the fruit of this seed? Verily, judgment in doctrine was wholly altered; order in discipline very sore changed; the love of good learning began suddenly to wax cold; the knowledge of the tongues (in spite of some that therein had flourished) was manifestly contemned; and so the way of right study purposely perverted, the choice of good authors of malice

[133] Grove arising out of the stumps of an older one.     [134] Clergy.
[135] Illiterate, inferior clergymen.
[136] Stole or scarf worn as a badge of ecclesiastical office.
[137] Breviary, and manual for calculating the dates of variable ecclesiastical feasts, such as Easter.

confounded. Old sophistry (I say not well), not old, but that new rotten sophistry, began to beard and shoulder logic in her own tongue; yea, I know that heads were cast together and counsel devised that Duns,[138] with all the rabble of barbarous questionists,[139] should have dispossessed of their place and rooms Aristotle, Plato, Tully, and Demosthenes, whom [140] good Master Redman and those two worthy stars of that university, Master Cheke and Master Smith, with their scholars, had brought to flourish as notable in Cambridge as ever they did in Greece and in Italy, and for the doctrine of those four, the four pillars of learning, Cambridge then giving no place to no university, neither in France, Spain, Germany, nor Italy. Also in outward behavior then began simplicity in apparel to be laid aside, courtly gallantness to be taken up; frugality in diet was privately misliked, town-going to good cheer openly used; honest pastimes, joined with labor, left off in the fields; unthrifty and idle games haunted corners and occupied the nights; contention in youth nowhere for learning, factions in the elders everywhere for trifles. All which miseries at length, by God's providence, had their end 16th November 1558.[141] Since which time the young spring hath shot up so fair as now there be in Cambridge again many goodly plants (as did well appear at the Queen's Majesty's late being there') which are like to grow to mighty great timber, to the honor of learning and great good of their country, if they may stand their time as the best plants there were wont to do, and if some old dotterel [142] trees, with standing overnigh them and dropping upon them, do not either hinder or crook their growing. Wherein my fear is the less,

[138] Duns Scotus.

[139] Scholastic philosophers, whose dialectic often proceeded by a method of propounding and answering questions.

[140] 1570: when.

[141] At the death of Queen Mary and accession of Queen Elizabeth, November 17, 1558.

[142] Top-decayed.

seeing so worthy a justice of an oyer [143] hath the present over-
sight of that whole chase,[144] who was himself sometime, in the
fairest spring that ever was there of learning, one of the forward-
est young plants in all that worthy College of St. John's, who
now by grace is grown to such greatness as, in the temperate
and quiet shade of his wisdom, next the providence of God and
goodness of one, in these our days *religio* for sincerity, *literae*
for order and advancement, *respublica* for happy and quiet
government have, to great rejoicing of all good men, specially
reposed [145] themselves.

Now to return to that question whether one, a few, many, or
all are to be followed, my answer shall be short: all, for him
that is desirous to know all; yea, the worst of all, as questionists
and all the barbarous nation of Schoolmen, help for one or
other consideration. But in every separate kind of learning and
study, by itself, ye must follow choicely a few and chiefly some
one, and that namely in our school of eloquence, either for pen
or talk. And as in portraiture and painting wise men choose not
that workman that can only make a fair hand or a well-fash-
ioned leg, but such one as can furnish up fully all the features
of the whole body of a man, woman, and child, and withal is
able too, by good skill, to give to every one of these three, in
their proper kind, the right form, the true figure, the natural
color that is fit and due to the dignity of a man, to the beauty of
a woman, to the sweetness of a young babe, even likewise do
we seek such one in our school to follow who is able always, in
all matters, to teach plainly, to delight pleasantly, and to carry
away by force of wise talk all that shall hear or read him, and is
so excellent indeed as wit is able or wish can hope to attain
unto. And this not only to serve in the Latin or Greek tongue,
but also in our own English language. But yet, because the

[143] Judge having power to hear and determine cases; that is, Sir William
Cecil, Chancellor of the University after 1559.
[144] Park land.     [145] Re-established.

providence of God hath left unto us in no other tongue, save only in the Greek and Latin tongue, the true precepts and perfect examples of eloquence, therefore must we seek in the authors only of those two tongues the true pattern of eloquence, if in any other mother tongue we look to attain either to perfect utterance of it ourselves or skillful judgment of it in others.

And now to know what author doth meddle only with some one piece and member of eloquence, and who doth perfectly make up the whole body, I will declare, as I can call to remembrance, the goodly talk that I have had oftentimes of the true difference of authors with that gentleman of worthy memory, my dearest friend and teacher of all the little poor learning I have, Sir John Cheke.

The true difference of authors is best known *per diversa genera dicendi* [146] that every one used. And therefore here I will divide *genus dicendi,* not into these three—*tenue, mediocre, et grande*—but as the matter of every author requireth, as:

$$in\ Genus \begin{cases} Poeticum \\ Historicum \\ Philosophicum \\ Oratorium. \end{cases}$$

These differ one from another in choice of words, in framing of sentences, in handling of arguments, and use of right form, figure, and number, proper and fit for every matter, and every one of these is diverse also in itself, as the first,

$$Poeticum,\ in \begin{cases} Comicum \\ Tragicum \\ Epicum \\ Melicum. \text{[147]} \end{cases}$$

And here whosoever hath been diligent to read advisedly over Terence, Seneca, Virgil, Horace, or else Aristophanes,

[146] Through the different kinds of discourse.     [147] Lyric.

Sophocles, Homer, and Pindar, and shall diligently mark the difference they use in propriety of words, in form of sentence, in handling of their matter, he shall easily perceive what is fit and *decorum* in every one, to the true use of perfect imitation. When Master Watson in St. John's College at Cambridge wrote his excellent tragedy of *Absalom*, Master Cheke, he, and I had many pleasant talks together in comparing the precepts of Aristotle and Horace *De arte poetica* with the examples of Euripides, Sophocles, and Seneca. Few men in writing of tragedies in our days have shot at this mark. Some in England, more in France, Germany, and Italy, also have written tragedies in our time, of the which not one, I am sure, is able to abide the true touch of Aristotle's precepts and Euripides' examples, save only two that ever I saw: Master Watson's *Absalom* and Georgius Buchananus' *Jephtha*. One man in Cambridge, well liked of many, but best liked of himself, was many times bold and busy to bring matters upon stages which he called tragedies. In one, whereby he looked to win his spurs, and whereat many ignorant fellows fast clapped their hands, he began the *protasis* [148] with *trochaiis octonariis,* [149] which kind of verse, as it is but seldom and rare in tragedies, so is it never used save only in *epitasi* [150] when the tragedy is highest and hottest and full of greatest troubles. I remember full well what Master Watson merely said unto me of his blindness and boldness in that behalf, although otherwise there passed much friendship between them. Master Watson had another manner care of perfection, with a fear and reverence of the judgment of the best learned; who to this day would never suffer yet his *Absalom* to go abroad, and that only because *in locis paribus* [151] *anapaestus*

---

[148] The opening part of the play.

[149] A verse consisting of eight trochaic feet or, better, four double trochees.

[150] The episode in a play where the plot begins to thicken.

[151] In a few places.

*139*

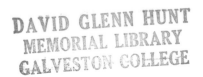

is twice or thrice used instead of *iambus*. A small fault, and such one as perchance would never be marked, no, neither in Italy nor France. This I write not so much to note the first or praise the last as to leave in memory of writing for good example to posterity what perfection in my [152] time was most diligently sought for in like manner, in all kind of learning, in that most worthy College of St. John's in Cambridge.

$$Historicum\ in \begin{cases} Diaria \\ Annales \\ Commentarios \\ Justam\ historiam. \end{cases}$$

For what propriety in words, simplicity in sentences, plainness, and light is comely for these kinds, Caesar and Livy, for the two last, are perfect examples of imitation; and for the two first the old patterns be lost, and as for some that be present and of late time, they be fitter to be read once for some pleasure than oft to be perused for any good imitation of them.

$$Philosophicum\ in \begin{cases} Sermonem,\ as\ Officia\ Ciceronis \\ et\ Ethicos\ Aristotelis \\ Contentionem.^{153} \end{cases}$$

As the dialogues of Plato, Xenophon, and Cicero, of which kind of learning, and right imitation thereof, Carolus Sigonius hath written of late both learnedly and eloquently,[154] but best of all my friend Joannes Sturmius in his commentaries upon *Gorgias Platonis*, which book I have in writing and is not yet set out in print.

$$Oratorium\ in \begin{cases} Humile \\ Mediocre \\ Sublime. \end{cases}$$

[152] 1570: any.
[153] Philosophical, into discourse, as the *De officiis* of Cicero and the *Nicomachean Ethics* of Aristotle; debate.
[154] Carlo Sigonio, *De dialogo liber* (Padua, 1561).

*140*

## The Ready Way to the Latin Tongue

Examples of these three in the Greek tongue be plentiful and perfect, as Lysias, Isocrates, and Demosthenes, and all three in only Demosthenes in divers orations, as *Contra Olympiodorum, In Leptinem, et Pro Ctesiphonte.* And true it is, that Hermogenes writeth of Demosthenes, that all forms of eloquence be perfect in him.[155] In Cicero's orations *medium et sublime* be most excellently handled, but *humile* in his orations is seldom seen; yet nevertheless in other books, as in some part of his *Offices,* and specially in *Partitionibus,* he is comparable *in hoc humili et disciplinabili genere* [156] even with the best that ever wrote in Greek. But of Cicero more fully in fitter place. And thus the true difference of styles in every author and every kind of learning may easily be known by this division:

$$\textit{in Genus} \begin{cases} \textit{Poeticum} \\ \textit{Historicum} \\ \textit{Philosophicum} \\ \textit{Oratorium.} \end{cases}$$

Which I thought in this place to touch only, not to prosecute at large, because, God willing, in the Latin tongue I will fully handle it in my book *De imitatione.*

Now to touch more particularly which of those authors that be now most commonly in men's hands will some afford you some piece of eloquence, and what manner a piece of eloquence, and what is to be liked and followed, and what to be misliked and eschewed in them, and how some again will furnish you fully withal, rightly and wisely considered, somewhat I will write as I have heard Sir John Cheke many times say.

The Latin tongue, concerning any part of pureness of it from

---

[155] Περὶ ἰδεῶν, I.i, *Rhetores Graeci,* ed. Christianus Walz, III (Stuttgart; Tübingen, 1834), 191–193, 197.

[156] In *De partitione oratoria,* he is comparable in this plain and instructional style.

the spring to the decay of the same, did not endure much longer than is the life of a well-aged man, scarce one hundred years from the time of the last Scipio Africanus and Laelius to the empire of Augustus. And it is notable that Velleius Paterculus writeth of Tully, how that the perfection of eloquence did so remain only in him and in his time, as before him were few which might much delight a man or after him any worthy admiration, but such as Tully might have seen and such as might have seen Tully.[157] And good cause why, for no perfection is durable. Increase hath a time, and decay likewise, but all perfect ripeness remaineth but a moment, as is plainly seen in fruits, plums, and cherries, but more sensibly in flowers, as roses and suchlike, and yet as truly in all greater matters. For what naturally can go no higher must naturally yield and stoop again.

Of this short time of any pureness of the Latin tongue, for the first forty year of it and all the time before, we have no piece of learning left save Plautus and Terence, with a little, rude, unperfect pamphlet of the elder Cato. And as for Plautus, except the schoolmaster be able to make wise and ware choice, first, in propriety of words, then, in framing of phrases and sentences, and, chiefly, in choice of honesty of matter, your scholar were better to play than to learn all that is in him. But surely if judgment for the tongue and direction for the manners be wisely joined with the diligent reading of Plautus, then truly Plautus, for that pureness of the Latin tongue in Rome when Rome did most flourish in well-doing, and so thereby in well-speaking also, is such a plentiful storehouse for common eloquence in mean matters and all private men's affairs as the Latin tongue for that respect hath not the like again. When I remember the worthy time of Rome wherein Plautus did live, I must needs honor the talk of that time which we see Plautus doth use.

---

[157] *Historiae Romanae libri duo,* I.xvii.3.

Terence is also a storehouse of the same tongue for another time following soon after, and although he be not so full and plentiful as Plautus is for multitude of matters and diversity of words, yet his words be chosen so purely, placed so orderly, and all his stuff so neatly packed up and wittily compassed in every place as, by all wise men's judgment, he is counted the cunninger workman and to have his shop, for the room that is in it, more finely appointed and trimlier ordered than Plautus' is.

Three things chiefly, both in Plautus and Terence, are to be specially considered: the matter; the utterance, the words; the meter. The matter in both is altogether within the compass of the meanest men's manners, and doth not stretch to anything of any great weight at all, but standeth chiefly in uttering the thoughts and conditions of hard fathers, foolish mothers, unthrifty young men, crafty servants, subtle bawds, and wily harlots, and so is much spent in finding out fine fetches and packing up pelting [158] matters, such as in London commonly come to the hearing of the masters of Bridewell. Here is base stuff for that scholar that should become hereafter either a good minister in religion or a civil gentleman in service of his prince and country, except the preacher do know such matters to confute them, when ignorance surely in all such things were better for a civil gentleman than knowledge. And thus, for matter, both Plautus and Terence be like mean painters that work by halves and be cunning only in making the worst part of the picture, as if one were skillful in painting the body of a naked person from the navel downward, but nothing else.

For word and speech Plautus is more plentiful and Terence more pure and proper, and for one respect Terence is to be embraced above all that ever wrote in his kind of argument: because it is well known by good record of learning, and that by Cicero's own witness, that some comedies bearing Terence's

[158] Trifling.

name were written by worthy Scipio and wise Laelius, and namely *Heautontimorumenos* and *Adelphi*.[159] And therefore as oft as I read those comedies, so oft doth sound in mine ear the pure, fine talk of Rome which was used by the flower of the worthiest nobility that ever Rome bred. Let the wisest man and best-learned that liveth read advisedly over the first scene of *Heautontimorumenos* and the first scene of *Adelphi*, and let him considerately judge whether it is the talk of a servile stranger born or rather even that mild, eloquent, wise speech which Cicero in *Brutus* doth so lively express in Laelius.[160] And yet nevertheless in all this good propriety of words and pureness of phrases which be in Terence, ye must not follow him always in placing of them, because for the meter's sake some words in him sometime be driven awry, which require a straiter placing in plain prose if ye will form, as I would ye should do, your speech and writing to that excellent perfectness which was only in Tully, or only in Tully's time.

The meter and verse of Plautus and Terence be very mean and not to be followed; which is not their reproach but the fault of the time wherein they wrote, when no kind of poetry in the Latin tongue was brought to perfection, as doth well appear in the fragments of Ennius, Caecilius,[161] and others, and evidently in Plautus and Terence, if these in Latin be compared with right skill with Homer, Euripides, Aristophanes, and other in Greek of like sort. Cicero himself doth complain of this unperfectness,[162] but more plainly Quintilian, saying: *In comoedia*

---

[159] *Epistolae ad Atticum*, VII.iii. Ascham inaccurately represents Cicero as crediting others with Terence's comedies. Cicero says here rather that "they used to ascribe (*putabantur*) his plays to Laelius." Likewise, Quintilian, who seems to be Ascham's source for the other attribution, remarks only that "they used to credit (*referantur*)" the plays to Scipio Africanus (*Institutio oratoria*, X.i.99).

[160] *Brutus*, xx.83–xxii.88.      [161] 1570: Cerilius.

[162] *Brutus*, xviii.71–xix.74.

*maxime claudicamus, et vix levem consequimur umbram,*[163] and most earnestly of all Horace in *Arte poetica,* which he doth, namely, *propter carmen iambicum,* and referreth all good students herein to the imitation of the Greek tongue, saying,

> *Exemplaria Graeca*
> *nocturna versate manu, versate diurna.*[164]

This matter maketh me gladly remember my sweet time spent at Cambridge and the pleasant talk which I had oft with Master Cheke and Master Watson of this fault, not only in the old Latin poets but also in our new English rhymers at this day. They wished, as Virgil and Horace were not wedded to follow the faults of former fathers (a shrewd [165] marriage in greater matters) but by right imitation of the perfect Grecians had brought poetry to perfectness also in the Latin tongue, that we Englishmen likewise would acknowledge and understand rightfully our rude, beggarly rhyming, brought first into Italy by Goths and Huns when all good verses and all good learning too were destroyed by them, and after carried into France and Germany, and at last received into England by men of excellent wit indeed but of small learning and less judgment in that behalf.

But now when men know the difference and have the examples both of the best and of the worst, surely to follow rather the Goths in rhyming than the Greeks in true versifying were even to eat acorns with swine when we may freely eat wheat bread amongst men. Indeed Chaucer, Thomas Norton of Bristol, my Lord of Surrey, Master Wyatt, Thomas Phaer, and other

---

[163] *Institutio oratoria,* X.i.99–100: "In comedy we limp badly, . . . we scarcely attain a faint shadow [of Greek comedy]."

[164] *Ars poetica,* 268–269: "Keep handling Greek models by night and day."

[165] Harmful.

gentlemen in translating Ovid, Palingenius, and Seneca have gone as far, to their great praise, as the copy they followed could carry them, but if such good wits and forward diligence had been directed to follow the best examples, and not have been carried by time and custom to content themselves with that barbarous and rude rhyming, amongst their other worthy praises which they have justly deserved this had not been the least, to be counted, amongst men of learning and skill, more like unto the Grecians than unto the Gothians in handling of their verse.

Indeed our English tongue, having in use chiefly words of one syllable which commonly be long, doth not well receive the nature of *carmen heroicum,* because *dactylus,* the aptest foot for that verse, containing one long and two short, is seldom therefore found in English and doth also rather stumble than stand upon *monosyllabis.* Quintilian in his learned chapter *"De compositione"* giveth this lesson *de monosyllabis* before me, and in the same place doth justly inveigh against all rhyming,[166] that if there be any who be angry with me for misliking of rhyming, may be angry for company, too, with Quintilian also for the same thing; and yet Quintilian had not so just cause to mislike of it then as men have at this day.

And although *carmen hexametrum* doth rather trot and hobble than run smoothly in our English tongue, yet I am sure our English tongue will receive *carmen iambicum* as naturally as either Greek or Latin. But for ignorance men cannot like, and for idleness men will not labor, to come to any perfectness at all. For as the worthy poets in Athens and Rome were more careful to satisfy the judgment of one learned than rash in pleasing the humor of a rude multitude, even so if men in England now had the like reverent regard to learning, skill, and judgment, and durst not presume to write except they came

---

[166] *Institutio oratoria,* IX.iv.42. Quintilian, however, is objecting here to overuse of rhyming sentences in prose, not to use of rhyme in poetry.

with the like learning and also did use like diligence in searching out not only just measure in every meter, as every ignorant person may easily do, but also true quantity in every foot and syllable, as only the learned shall be able to do, and as the Greeks and Romans were wont to do, surely then rash, ignorant heads, which now can easily reckon up fourteen syllables and easily stumble on every rhyme, either durst not, for lack of such learning, or else would not, in avoiding such labor, be so busy as everywhere they be, and shops in London should not be so full of lewd and rude rhymes as commonly they are. But now the ripest of tongue be readiest to write, and many daily in setting out books and ballads make great show of blossoms and buds, in whom is neither root of learning nor fruit of wisdom at all. Some that make Chaucer in English and Petrarch in Italian their gods in verses, and yet be not able to make true difference what is a fault and what is a just praise in those two worthy wits, will much mislike this my writing. But such men be even like followers of Chaucer and Petrarch as one here in England did follow Sir Thomas More, who, being most unlike unto him in wit and learning, nevertheless in wearing his gown awry upon the one shoulder, as Sir Thomas More was wont to do, would needs be counted like unto him.

This misliking of rhyming beginneth not now of any new-fangled singularity but hath been long misliked of many, and that of men of greatest learning and deepest judgment. And such that defend it do so either for lack of knowledge what is best or else of very envy that any should perform that in learning whereunto they, as I said before, either for ignorance cannot, or for idleness will not, labor to attain unto.

And you that praise this rhyming, because ye neither have reason why to like it nor can show learning to defend it, yet I will help you with the authority of the oldest and learnedest time. In Greece, when poetry was even at [167] the highest pitch

[167] 1570: as.

of perfectness, one Simias Rhodius of a certain singularity wrote a book in rhyming Greek verses, naming it 'Ωόν, containing the fable how Jupiter in likeness of a swan gat that egg upon Leda whereof came Castor, Pollux, and fair Helena.[168] This book was so liked that it had few to read it, but none to follow it, but was presently contemned and soon after both author and book so forgotten by men and consumed by time as scarce the name of either is kept in memory of learning. And the like folly was never followed of any many hundred years after until the Huns and Gothians, and other barbarous nations, of ignorance and singularity did revive the same folly again.

The noble lord Thomas [169] Earl of Surrey, first of all Englishmen in translating the fourth book of Virgil, and Gonsalvo Perez, that excellent learned man and secretary to King Philip of Spain, in translating the Ulysses of Homer out of Greek into Spanish,[170] have both by good judgment avoided the fault of rhyming, yet neither of them hath fully hit perfect and true versifying. Indeed, they observe just number and even feet, but here is the fault, that their feet be feet without joints, that is to say, not distinct by true quantity of syllables; and so such feet be but numb feet and be even as unfit for a verse to turn and run roundly withal as feet of brass or wood be unwieldy to go well withal. And as a foot of wood is a plain show of a manifest maim,[171] even so feet, in our English versifying, without quantity and joints, be sure signs that the verse is either born deformed, unnatural, and lame, and so very unseemly to look upon, except to men that be goggle-eyed themselves.

---

[168] *The Greek Bucolic Poets* [Loeb], Simias, III. As Mayor points out, the poem is neither in rhymed verses nor about Leda, but like the same poet's "Axe" and "Wings" represents a tour de force of patterned versifying that resembles specimens appearing in the works of George Herbert.

[169] 1570: *Th.* Earle. Possibly Ascham or the printer confused the poet Henry with his father Thomas, but Mayor's footnote emendation to "Th'Earl" is also plausible.

[170] *La Odisea de Homero* (Antwerp, 1553).    [171] 1570: maine.

## The Ready Way to the Latin Tongue

The spying of this fault now is not the curiosity of English eyes, but even the good judgment also of the best that write in these days in Italy, and namely of that worthy Sienese Felice Figliucci, who, writing upon Aristotle's *Ethics* so excellently in Italian as never did yet anyone, in mine opinion, either in Greek or Latin, amongst other things doth most earnestly inveigh against the rude rhyming of verses in that tongue. And whensoever he expresseth Aristotle's precepts with any example out of Homer or Euripides, he translateth them, not after the rhymes of Petrarch, but into such kind of perfect verse, with like feet and quantity of syllables, as he found them before in the Greek tongue, exhorting earnestly all the Italian nation to leave off their rude barbarousness in rhyming and follow diligently the excellent Greek and Latin examples in true versifying.[172]

And you that be able to understand no more than ye find in the Italian tongue, and never went farther than the school of Petrarch and Ariostus abroad, or else of Chaucer at home, though you have pleasure to wander blindly still in your foul wrong way, envy not others that seek, as wise men have done before them, the fairest and rightest way; or else, beside the just reproach of malice, wise men shall truly judge that you do so, as I have said and say yet again unto you, because either for idleness ye will not, or for ignorance ye cannot, come by no better yourself.

And therefore even as Virgil and Horace deserve most worthy praise, that they, spying the unperfectness in Ennius and Plautus, by true imitation of Homer and Euripides brought poetry to the same perfectness in Latin as it was in Greek, even so those that by the same way would benefit their tongue and

---

[172] *De la filosofia morale libri dieci. Sopra li dieci dell'Ethica d'Aristotile* (Rome, 1551). In more than two dozen places Figliucci translates Greek verses into unrhymed Italian meters that try to imitate the original faithfully; he defends his practice in his "Proemio," (sig. Av) and again immediately after his first effort at translation (p. 19).

country deserve rather thanks than dispraise in that behalf. And I rejoice that even poor England prevented [173] Italy, first, in spying out, then, in seeking to amend, this fault in learning.

And here for my pleasure I purpose a little, by the way, to play and sport with my master Tully, from whom commonly I am never wont to dissent. He himself, for this point of learning, in his verses doth halt a little, by his leave. He could not deny it if he were alive, nor those defend him now that love him best. This fault I lay to his charge because once it pleased him, though somewhat merrily, yet overuncourteously, to rail upon poor England, objecting both extreme beggary and mere barbarousness unto it, writing thus unto his friend Atticus: "There is not one scruple of silver in that whole isle, or anyone that knoweth either learning or letter." [174]

But now, Master Cicero, blessed be God and his son Jesu Christ whom you never knew, except it were as it pleased him to lighten you by some shadow, as covertly in one place ye confess, saying, *Veritatis tantum umbram confectamur,* as your master Plato did before you,[175] blessed be God, I say, that sixteen hundred year after you were dead and gone it may truly be said that for silver there is more comely plate in one city of England than is in four of the proudest cities in all Italy, and take Rome for one of them. And for learning, beside the knowledge of all learned tongues and liberal sciences, even your own books, Cicero, be as well read, and your excellent eloquence is as well liked and loved and as truly followed in England at this

[173] Anticipated.

[174] *Epistolae ad Atticum,* IV.xxvii: *Neque argenti scripulum esse ullum in illa insula neque . . . ex quibus nullos puto te litteris aut musicis eruditos exspectare.*

[175] "We have obtained only a shadow of the truth." Cicero's actual words have to do with mankind's having "a mere outline sketch" rather than any "substantial, life-like image of true Law and genuine Justice" (*De officiis,* III.xvii.69). The reference to Plato is to the famous passage on the images in the cave (*Republic,* VII.515C).

day, as it is now, or ever was since your own time, in any place of Italy, either at Arpinum, where ye were born, or else at Rome, where ye were brought up. And a little to brag with you, Cicero, where you yourself, by your leave, halted in some point of learning in your own tongue, many in England at this day go straight up, both in true skill and right doing therein.

This I write, not to reprehend Tully, whom above all other I like and love best, but to excuse Terence because in his time, and a good while after, poetry was never perfected in Latin until by true imitation of the Grecians it was at length brought to perfection, and also thereby to exhort the goodly wits of England which, apt by nature, and willing by desire, give themselves to poetry, that they, rightly understanding the barbarous bringing-in of rhymes, would labor, as Virgil and Horace did in Latin, to make perfect also this point of learning in our English tongue.

And thus much for Plautus and Terence for matter, tongue, and meter, what is to be followed and what to be eschewed in them.

After Plautus and Terence, no writing remaineth until Tully's time except a few short fragments of Lucius Crassus' excellent wit, here and there recited of Cicero for example's sake, whereby the lovers of learning may the more lament the loss of such a worthy wit.

And although the Latin tongue did fair bloom and blossom in Lucius Crassus and Marcus Antonius, yet in Tully's time only, and in Tully himself chiefly, was the Latin tongue fully ripe and grown to the highest pitch of all perfection.

And yet in the same time it began to fade and stoop, as Tully himself in *Brutus de claris oratoribus* with weeping words doth witness.[176]

And because amongst them of that time there was some

[176] Vi.21–22.

difference, good reason is that of them of that time should be made right choice also. And yet let the best Ciceronian in Italy read Tully's familiar epistles advisedly over, and I believe he shall find small difference for the Latin tongue, either in propriety of words or framing of the style, betwixt Tully and those that write unto him, as Servius Sulpicius, Aulus Caecina, Marcus Caelius, Marcus *et* Decimus Brutus, Asinius Pollio, Lucius Plancus, and divers other. Read the epistles of Lucius Plancus in tenth *libro* and for an assay that epistle, namely to the consuls and whole senate (the eighth epistle in number), and what could be either more eloquently or more wisely written, yea, by Tully himself, a man may justly doubt. These men and Tully lived all in one time, were like in authority, not unlike in learning and study, which might be just causes of this their equality in writing; and yet surely they neither were indeed, nor yet were counted in men's opinions, equal with Tully in that faculty. And how is the difference hid in his epistles? Verily, as the cunning of an expert seaman, in a fair, calm, fresh river, doth little differ from the doing of a meaner workman therein, even so, in the short cut of a private letter where matter is common, words easy, and order not much diverse, small show of difference can appear. But where Tully doth set up his sail of eloquence in some broad, deep argument, carried with full tide and wind of his wit and learning, all other may rather stand and look after him than hope to overtake him, what course soever he hold, either in fair or foul. Four men only when the Latin tongue was full ripe be left unto us, who in that time did flourish and did leave to posterity the fruit of their wit and learning: Varro, Sallust, Caesar, and Cicero. When I say these four only I am not ignorant that even in the same time most excellent poets, deserving well of the Latin tongue, as Lucretius, Catullus, Virgil, and Horace, did write. But because in this little book I purpose to teach a young scholar to go, not to dance, to speak, not to sing—when poets indeed, namely *epici* and *lyrici*, as these be, are fine dancers and trim singers, but *oratores* and *historici* be those comely goers and fair and wise speakers of whom I wish my scholar to wait upon first, and after, in good order and due time, to be brought forth to the singing and dancing school—and for this consideration do I name these four to be the only writers of that time.

### Varro

Varro, in his books *De lingua Latina et Analogia*, as these be left mangled and patched unto us, doth not enter there into any great depth of eloquence, but as one carried in a small, low vessel himself very nigh the common shore, not much unlike the fishermen of Rye and herring men of Yarmouth, who deserve, by common men's opinion, small commendation for any cunning sailing at all, yet nevertheless in those books of Varro good and necessary stuff for that mean kind of argument be very well and learnedly gathered together.

His books of husbandry are much to be regarded and diligently to be read, not only for the propriety but also for the plenty of good words, in all country and husbandmen's affairs, which cannot be had by so good authority out of any other author, either of so good a time or of so great learning, as out of Varro. And yet because he was fourscore year old when he wrote those books, the form of his style there, compared with Tully's writing, is but even the talk of a spent old man whose words commonly fall out of his mouth, though very wisely, yet hardly and coldly, and more heavily also than some ears can well bear, except only for age and authority's sake. And perchance, in a rude country argument, of purpose and judgment he rather used the speech of the country than talk of the city.

And so for matter's sake his words sometime be somewhat rude and, by the imitation of the elder Cato, old and out of use, and being deep stepped in age, by negligence some words do so scape and fall from him in those books as be not worth the taking-up by him that is careful to speak or write true Latin, as that sentence in him: *Romani, in pace a rusticis alebantur, et in bello ab his tuebantur.*[177] A good student must be therefore careful and diligent to read with judgment over even those authors which did write in the most perfect time, and let him not be afraid to try them, both in propriety of words and form of style, by the touchstone of Caesar and Cicero, whose purity was never foiled,[178] no, not by the sentence [179] of those that loved them worst.

All lovers of learning may sore lament the loss of those books of Varro which he wrote in his young and lusty years, with good leisure and great learning of all parts of philosophy, of the goodliest arguments pertaining both to the commonwealth and private life of man, as *De ratione studii et educandis liberis,* which book is oft recited and much praised in the fragments of Nonius, even for authority's sake. He wrote most diligently and largely also the whole history of the state of Rome, the mysteries of their whole religion, their laws, customs, and government in peace, their manners and whole discipline in war, and this is not my guessing, as one indeed that never saw those books, but even the very judgment and plain testimony of Tully himself, who knew and read those books, in these words: *Tu aetatem patriae, tu descriptiones temporum, tu sacrorum, tu sacerdotum jura, tu domesticam, tu bellicam disciplinam, tu sedem regionum, locorum, tu omnium divinarum humanarumque rerum nomina, genera, officia, causas aperuisti, etc.*[180]

[177] Quoted with slight changes from Varro, *De re rustica,* III.i.4: "In peace they were fed by the country folk and in war defended by them."

[178] Defiled, tarnished.     [179] Opinion.

[180] "You have revealed the age of our native city, the chronology of its history, the laws of its religion and its priesthood, its civil and its military institutions, the topography of its districts and its sites, the terminology, classification and moral and rational basis of all our religious and secular institutions," etc. (*Academica,* I.iii.9). Reprinted by permission of the publishers and the Loeb Classical Library from Cicero, *De natura deorum; Academica,* trans. H. Rackham (Cambridge, Mass.: Harvard University Press, 1961), p. 419.

## The Ready Way to the Latin Tongue

But this great loss of Varro is a little recompensed by the happy coming of Dionysius Halicarnassaeus to Rome in Augustus' days, who, getting the possession of Varro's library, out of that treasure house of learning did leave unto us some fruit of Varro's wit and diligence, I mean his goodly books *De antiquitatibus Romanorum*. Varro was so esteemed for his excellent learning as Tully himself had a reverence to his judgment in all doubts of learning. And Antonius Triumvir, his enemy, and of a contrary faction, who had power to kill and banish whom he listed,[181] when Varro's name amongst others was brought in a schedule unto him to be noted to death he took his pen and wrote his warrant of safeguard with these most goodly words: *Vivat Varro vir doctissimus*.[182] In later time, no man knew better, nor liked nor loved more, Varro's learning than did St. Augustine, as they do well understand that have diligently read over his learned books *De civitate Dei*, where he hath this most notable sentence: "When I see how much Varro wrote, I marvel much that ever he had any leisure to read, and when I perceive how many things he read, I marvel more that ever he had any leisure to write," etc.[183]

And surely if Varro's books had remained to posterity as, by God's providence, the most part of Tully's did, then truly the Latin tongue might have made good comparison with the Greek.

### Sallust

Sallust is a wise and worthy writer, but he requireth a learned reader and a right considerer of him. My dearest friend

---

[181] Wished.

[182] "Let the most learned man Varro live." Ascham's story seems apocryphal, for, according to Aulus Gellius, Varro was proscribed (*The Attic Nights*, III.x.17).

[183] "*Varro, qui tam multa legit ut aliquid ei scribere vacuisse miremur; tam multa scripsit quam multa vix quemquam legere potuisse credamus*," etc. (VI.ii).

and best master that ever I had or heard in learning, Sir John Cheke, such a man as, if I should live to see England breed the like again, I fear I should live overlong, did once give me a lesson for Sallust which, as I shall never forget myself, so is it worthy to be remembered of all those that would come to perfect judgment of the Latin tongue. He said that Sallust was not very fit for young men to learn out of him the purity of the Latin tongue, because he was not the purest in propriety of words, nor choicest in aptness of phrases, nor the best in framing of sentences, and therefore is his writing (said he) neither plain for the matter nor sensible for men's understanding. "And what is the cause thereof, sir?" quoth I. "Verily," said he, "because in Sallust's writing is more art than nature, and more labor than art, and in his labor also too much toil, as it were, with an uncontented care to write better than he could, a fault common to very many men. And therefore he doth not express the matter lively and naturally with common speech as ye see Xenophon doth in Greek, but it is carried and driven forth artificially, after too learned a sort, as Thucydides doth in his orations." "And how cometh it to pass," said I, "that Caesar's and Cicero's talk is so natural and plain and Sallust's writing so artificial and dark, when all they three lived in one time?" "I will freely tell you my fancy herein," said he. "Surely Caesar and Cicero, beside a singular prerogative of natural eloquence given unto them by God, both two, by use of life, were daily orators amongst the common people and greatest counselors in the senate house, and therefore gave themselves to use such speech as the meanest should well understand and the wisest best allow, following carefully that good counsel of Aristotle: *loquendum ut multi, sapiendum ut pauci.*[184] Sallust was no such man, neither for will to goodness nor skill by learning, but ill-

---

[184] "Speaking like the many, understanding like the few." In various forms, a commonplace of the Renaissance, not to be found specifically in Aristotle's *Rhetoric* but perhaps suggested by his comments on the use of language in III.1404B.

given by nature, and made worse by bringing-up, spent the
most part of his youth very misorderly in riot and lechery in the
company of such who, never giving their mind to honest doing,
could never inure their tongue to wise speaking. But at last
coming to better years and buying wit at the dearest hand, that
is, by long experience of the hurt and shame that cometh of
mischief, moved by the counsel of them that were wise and
carried by the example of such as were good, first fell to
honesty of life and after to the love of study and learning, and
so became so new a man that Caesar, being dictator, made him
praetor in Numidia, where he, absent from his country and not
inured with the common talk of Rome, but shut up in his study
and bent wholly to reading, did write the story of the Romans.
And for the better accomplishing of the same he read Cato and
Piso in Latin for gathering of matter and truth, and Thucydides
in Greek for the order of his story and furnishing of his style.
Cato (as his time required) had more truth for the matter than
eloquence for the style. And so Sallust, by gathering truth out
of Cato, smelleth much of the roughness of his style, even as a
man that eateth garlic for health shall carry away with him the
savor of it also whether he will or not. And yet the use of old
words is not the greatest cause of Sallust's roughness and darkness. There be in Sallust some old words indeed, as *patrare
bellum, ductare exercitum,* well noted by Quintilian and very
much misliked of him,[185] and *supplicium* for *supplicatio,* a word
smelling of an older store than the other two so misliked by
Quintilian. And yet is that word also in Varro, speaking of oxen
thus: *Boves ad victimas faciunt, atque ad deorum supplicia,*
and a few old words more.[186] Read Sallust and Tully advisedly

[185] *Institutio oratoria,* VIII.iii.44. But Quintilian objects to these phrases,
which mean literally "to bring the war to an end" and "to lead an army,"
only because in popular usage they had taken on an obscene meaning.

[186] "They use the cattle for sacrificial victims, and solemn offerings to
the gods" (*De re rustica,* II.v.10).

together and in words ye shall find small difference; yea, Sallust is more given to new words than to old, though some old writers say the contrary, as *claritudo* for *gloria, exacte* for *perfecte, facundia* for *eloquentia.*[187] These two last words *exacte* and *facundia,* now in every man's mouth, be never (as I do remember) used of Tully, and therefore I think they be not good, for surely Tully, speaking everywhere so much of the matter of eloquence, would not so precisely have abstained from the word *facundia* if it had been good, that is, proper for the tongue and common for men's use. I could be long in reciting many suchlike, both old and new words, in Sallust, but in very deed neither oldness nor newness of words maketh the greatest difference betwixt Sallust and Tully, but, first, strange phrases made of good Latin words, but framed after the Greek tongue, which be neither choicely borrowed of them nor properly used by him, then, a hard composition and crooked framing of his words and sentences, as a man would say, 'English talk placed and framed outlandishlike.' As, for example, first, in phrases *nimius et animus* be two used words, yet *homo nimius animi* [188] is an unused phrase. *Vulgus, et amat, et fieri* be as common and well-known words as may be in the Latin tongue, yet *id quod vulgo amat fieri* for *solet fieri* [189] is but a strange and Greekish kind of writing. *Ingens et vires* be proper words, yet

---

[187] Ascham's objection to these words—meaning respectively *fame, perfectly, eloquence*—reflects his general distaste for such writers as Sallust and Tacitus, whose style represented to him a decline from the perfection of Cicero. Sallust, incidentally, does not use the word *exacte.*

[188] The words, in Fragment IV.vi.74, of Sallust's *Histories,* are *Impotens et nimius animi est:* "He is headstrong and excessive in passion" (*Catilina, Iugurtha, Historiarum fragmenta,* ed. Fridericus Kritzius [Leipzig, 1856], p. 332).

[189] Quintilian (IX.iii.17) cites *vulgus amat fieri*—"such things as the people love to see done"—as an example of Sallust's Grecism, but neither Ascham's nor Quintilian's version of the phrase appears in Sallust's extant writings.

# The Ready Way to the Latin Tongue

*vir ingens virium* [190] is an unproper kind of speaking; and so be likewise

> *aeger consilii,*
> *promptissimus belli,*
> *territus animi,* [191]

and many suchlike phrases in Sallust, borrowed, as I said, not choicely out of Greek, and used therefore unproperly in Latin. Again, in whole sentences, where the matter is good, the words proper and plain, yet the sense is hard and dark, and namely in his prefaces and orations, [192] wherein he used most labor, which fault is likewise in Thucydides in Greek, of whom Sallust hath taken the greatest part of his darkness. For Thucydides likewise wrote his story, not at home in Greece but abroad in Italy, and therefore smelleth of a certain outlandish kind of talk, strange to them of Athens and diverse from their writing that lived in Athens and Greece and wrote the same time that Thucydides did, as Lysias, Xenophon, Plato, and Isocrates, the purest and plainest writers that ever wrote in any tongue and best examples for any man to follow whether he write Latin, Italian, French, or English. Thucydides also seemeth in his writing not so much benefited by nature as holpen [193] by art and carried forth by desire, study, labor, toil, and overgreat curiosity, who spent twenty-seven years in writing his eight books of his history. Sallust likewise wrote out of his country and followed the faults of Thucydides too much, and borroweth of him some kind of writing which the Latin tongue cannot well bear, as

---

[190] *Ingens ipse virium atque animi:* "He is mighty in strength and also in spirit" (*Historiarum fragmenta*, III.ii.10).

[191] "Feeble in judgment; all too eager for war; terrified in spirit" (*ibid.,* IV.vi.76, II.ii.18, IV.i.8, respectively). In all these phrases, Ascham seems to be objecting to an apparently locative use of the genitive case.

[192] 1570: oration.      [193] Helped.

*casus nominativus* in divers places *absolute positus*,[194] as in that place of *Jugurtha*, speaking *de Leptitanis: Itaque ab imperatore facile quae petebant adepti, missae sunt eo cohortes Ligurum quattuor*.[195] This thing in participles, used so oft in Thucydides and other Greek authors too, may better be borne withal, but Sallust useth the same more strangely and boldly, as in these words: *Multis sibi quisque imperium petentibus*.[196] I believe the best grammarian in England can scarce give a good rule why *quisque*, the nominative case without any verb, is so thrust up amongst so many oblique cases. Some man perchance will smile and laugh to scorn this my writing, and call it idle curiosity thus to busy myself in pickling[197] about these small points of grammar, not fit for my age, place, and calling to trifle in. I trust that man, be he never so great in authority, never so wise and learned either by other men's judgment or his own opinion, will yet think that he is not greater in England than Tully was at Rome, nor yet wiser nor better learned than Tully was himself, who, at the pitch of threescore years, in the midst of the broil betwixt Caesar and Pompey, when he knew not whither to send wife and children, which way to go, where to hide himself, yet in an earnest letter, amongst his earnest counsels for those heavy times concerning both the common state of his country and his own private great affairs, he was neither unmindful nor ashamed to reason at large and learn gladly of Atticus a less point of grammar than these be, noted of me in Sallust, as whether he should write *ad Piraeea, in Piraeea,* or *in Piraeum,* or *Piraeum sine praepositione.* And in those heavy

---

[194] The nominative case used, instead of the ablative, in an absolute sense.

[195] "Therefore what they were petitioning for was readily granted by the commander-in-chief, from whom four cohorts of Ligurians were sent to their aid" (lxxvii.4).

[196] "There were many on every hand who aspired to succeed him" (xviii.3).

[197] Piddling.

times he was so careful to know this small point of grammar that he addeth these words: *Si hoc mihi persolveris, magna me molestia liberaris.*[198] If Tully, at that age, in that authority, in that care for his country, in that jeopardy for himself and extreme necessity of his dearest friends, being also the prince of eloquence himself, was not ashamed to descend to these low points of grammar in his own natural tongue, what should scholars do, yea, what should any man do, if he do think well-doing better than ill-doing and had rather be perfect than mean, sure than doubtful, to be what he should be indeed, not seem what he is not in opinion? He that maketh perfectness in the Latin tongue his mark must come to it by choice and certain knowledge, not stumble upon it by chance and doubtful ignorance, and the right steps to reach unto it be these, linked thus orderly together: aptness of nature, love of learning, diligence in right order, constancy with pleasant moderation, and always to learn of them that be best; and so shall you judge as they that be wisest." And these be those rules which worthy Master Cheke did impart unto me concerning Sallust and the right judgment of the Latin tongue.

### Caesar

Caesar, for the little of him that is left unto us, is like the half face of a Venus, the other part of the head being hidden, the body and the rest of the members unbegun, yet so excellently done by Apelles as all men may stand still to maze [199] and muse upon it and no man step forth with any hope to perform the like.

His seven books *De bello Gallico* and three *De bello civili* be

[198] *Epistolae ad Atticum,* VII.iii: "If you can solve this problem for me [in what form to write the phrase 'to the Piraeus'], you will free me from a great difficulty."
[199] Marvel.

written so wisely for the matter, so eloquently for the tongue, that neither his greatest enemies could ever find the least note of partiality in him (a marvelous wisdom of a man, namely, writing of his own doings), nor yet the best judgers of the Latin tongue, nor the most envious lookers upon other men's writings, can say any other but all things be most perfectly done by him.

Brutus, Calvus, and Calidius, who found fault with Tully's fullness in words and matter, and that rightly, for Tully did both confess it and mend it, yet in Caesar they neither did nor could find the like or any other fault.

And therefore thus justly may I conclude of Caesar that where in all other, the best that ever wrote in any time or in any tongue, in Greek or Latin (I except neither Plato, Demosthenes, nor Tully), some fault is justly noted, in Caesar only could never yet fault be found.

Yet nevertheless, for all this perfect excellency in him, yet it is but in one member of eloquence, and that but of one side neither, when we must look for that example to follow which hath a perfect head, a whole body, forward and backward, arms and legs and all.[200]

[200] Obviously Cicero, who apparently would have been dealt with at length in the portion of *The Schoolmaster* that was either not finished or lost.

*FINIS*

# INDEX

# Index

Bryan, Sir Francis, 109
Bucer, Martin, xix
Buchanan, George, 139
Budé, Guillaume, 16, 122

Caecilius, 144
Caesar, Julius, 13, 53, 79, 90, 152, 156–157, 160; a model of purest Latin, xxxiv, 77–78, 94, 116, 154, 161–162; as historian, xxxvii, 140, 161–162
Camerarius, Joachim, 123
Canterus, Gulielmus, 112
Carion, Johann, 112
Castalion, Sébastien, 88
Castiglione, Baldassare, 55
Cato, 142, 153, 157
Catullus, xxxviii, 124, 152
Cecil, William, Lord Burghley, xiii, 3, 5–7, 10–11, 137
Celsus, 84
Charles V, Emperor, xix, xx, xxiv
Chaucer, Geoffrey, 145, 147, 149
Cheke, Sir John, xxviii, 26, 45, 133; influence on Ascham, 9, 10, 118, 128, 138, 141, 145; judgment on Sallust, 156–161; leadership at Cambridge, xiv–xv, 56, 131, 136
Cholmley, Sir Roger, 50–51
Chrysostom, St. John, 45
Chytraeus, David, 112
Cicero, xvii, xxvi, xxxii–xxxvii passim, 10, 15, 48, 79, 85–98 passim, 106, 110, 116–130 passim, 136, 152–162 passim; Brutus, 13, 111, 113–114, 122, 144, 151; De amicitia, 77, 80; De finibus, 80, 96; De legibus, 17; De officiis, 70, 96–97, 140, 141, 150; De oratore, xxv, 14, 16, 17, 29, 42, 83–84, 111, 119–122; De partitione oratoria, 93, 141; De senectute, 77, 86;

Cicero (cont.)
epistles, 14, 16, 77, 78, 86, 119–121, 150–152, 161; orations, 19, 92, 103–104, 141; Orator, 122
Cortesi, Paolo, 123
Cox, Bishop Richard, 7
Cuspinianus, Joannes, 33
Cyprian, St., xvii

Demades, 48
Demosthenes, xvii, 87, 89, 136, 162; as an ideal model, xxxvi, xxxvii, 93, 95, 101, 110, 128–129, 141; imitated by Cicero, 91, 117, 125, 127, 130; orations against Aeschines, xxi, 7, 48, 111
Denny, Sir Anthony, 80
Dinarchus, 48
Dio Prusaeus, 86
Dionysius Halicarnasseus, 29, 95; as historian, 129, 130, 155; on composition, 86, 122
Donatus, Aelius, 112
Du Bellay, Cardinal Jean, 49
Du Bellay, Guillaume, Sieur de Langey, 49
Duns Scotus, 136

Edward VI, King, xvi, xviii, xx, 55
Elizabeth I, Queen, xiii, 5, 91, 136; scholarly attainments, xxxiii, 56, 87; tutored by Ascham, xvi–xxi passim, 7, 9, 80–81, 107
Elstob, William, xxxv
Elyot, Sir Thomas, xxvii, xxix; The Governor, xi–xii
Ennius, 144, 149
Eobanus Hessus, Helius, 117, 128, 130
Ephorus, 48

# Index

Erasmus, Desiderius, xv, xxiv, 51, 108, 127; on imitation, 117, 122
Estienne, Henri, 128, 130
Euclid, 48
Eunomius, 84
Euripides, xv, 48, 130; as exemplary dramatist, xxxviii, 129, 139, 144, 149

Ferrières, Jean de, Vidame of Chartres, 49
Figliucci, Felice, 149
Francis I, King, 49

Galen, 23
Gardiner, Bishop Stephen, xx, 113
Goodrich, Richard, 9
Grey, Lady Jane, xiii, xix, xxviii, xxix, 35–36
Grindal, William, xvi
Guarino, Battista, xxiii

Haddon, Walter, 5–7, 10, 91, 109, 126, 131
Hall, Edward, 108
Hampton, Bernard, 5
Helvidius, 84
Hermogenes, 89, 141
Herodotus, xv, xxxvii, 48, 95, 112
Hesiod, 65, 102, 104
Heynes, Simon, 133
Hoby, Sir Thomas, 55
Homer, xxxvii, 70, 129, 139; as prince of poets, 54, 102, 144, 149; Iliad, 89, 99–100; Odyssey, 61–65, 148; Virgil's imitation of, xxxvi, 117, 124–125, 130
Horace, 62, 104, 129, 138, 152; Ars Poetica, 17, 54, 108, 139, 145; as reformer of Latin poetry, 149, 151; imitation of Pindar, 117, 130; Satires, 71, 105
Horman, William, 14, 107

Isaeus, 48
Isocrates, 30, 37, 48, 122; Areopagiticus, 46–47; as model, xvii, 87, 127–130 passim, 141, 159; De laudibus Helenae, 108; To Demonicus, 29

Jerome, St., 84
Johnson, Samuel, xxxvi
Jonson, Ben, xxxix
Joyce, James, xxviii

Kempis, Thomas à, 88

Livy, xv, xvii, xxxvii, 106, 129; as model, 78, 79, 104, 140; imitation of Polybius, 130
Locke, John, xxxv
Lombard, Peter, 107
Longueil, Christophe de, 122, 125
Lucian, 108
Lucretius, 152
Luther, Martin, 71, 110
Lycurgus, 48
Lysias, 48, 141, 159

Machiavelli, Niccolò, 72
Macrobius, 117, 128, 130
Maltravers, Lord Henry, 55
Mary Tudor, Queen, xx, 136
Mason, Sir John, 5, 6
Maximilian I, Emperor, 33
Melanchthon, Philip, xvii, 92–93, 107, 112, 123
Menander, 48, 117
Metcalfe, Nicholas, xiv, 132–134
Mildmay, Sir Walter, 5, 7
Milton, John, xxiii, xxxix
Montaigne, Michel de, xxix
More, St. Thomas, xv, 147
Morison, Sir Richard, xix
Morte Darthur, 68–69
Mountjoy, Charles Blount, 5th Lord, xv

165

# Index

166

# Index

167